Writing
Excel Macros

Elna R. Tymes
with Charles E. Prael

COMPUTE! Books
Radnor, Pennsylvania

Editor: Robert Bixby

Printed in the United States of America

10 9 8 7 6 5 4 3 2 1

COMPUTE! Books, Post Office Box 5406, Greensboro, North Carolina 27403, (919) 275-9809, is a Capital Cities/ABC, Inc. company and is not associated with any manufacturer of personal computers. *1-2-3* is a registered trademark of Lotus Development Corporation. *Excel* is a trademark of Microsoft Corporation. PC, PC XT and PC AT are registered trademarks of International Business Machines Corporation. Macintosh is a trademark licensed to Apple Computer, Inc.

Library of Congress Cataloging-in-Publication Data

Tymes, Elna.
   Writing Excel Macros/Elna R. Tymes with Charles E. Prael.
      p.   cm.
   Includes index.
   ISBN 0-87455-184-6
      1. Microsoft Excel (Computer program) 2. Computer software—
Development. 3. Business—Data processing.   I. Prael, Charles E.
II. Title.
HF5548.4.M523T95   1989
650'.028'55369—dc19   88-63197
                                                                CIP

Contents

Foreword

If you're a businessperson who has used *Excel*—whether on the PC or the Macintosh—you've probably developed a healthy respect for the power in this remarkable spreadsheet program. And this power is available not only to the people who design applications for *Excel*, but also to you. Opening up *Excel* and creating your own powerful macros is much simpler than you might imagine, but you'll need a guide to get started, particularly if you don't have a strong background in programming.

This is why Elna Tymes and Charles Prael put this book together. In *Writing Excel Macros*, the authors explode the myth that you have to be a programming genius to work with programming. All it takes is some thoughtful planning and the knowledge to open and operate on macro sheets. *Excel* even features a program recorder that can copy every action you make and create a program to mimic your keystrokes and mouse movements.

In this book you'll learn basic concepts about using macros, such as creating macros and implementing them efficiently; creating and using functions and formulas; editing, testing, and documenting your macros; using the Recorder; programming concepts; working with non-*Excel* files; creating automatic macros; using customizing techniques; and handling data and variables.

Excel is a software phenomenon. It has earned itself wide popularity partly because it's so malleable and friendly, but mostly because it's very powerful. Casual users appreciate its friendliness, flexibility, and speed. Power users respect its ponderous programming capabilities.

Writing Excel Macros will start you writing macros quickly. For your convenience, this book contains a quick reference guide to macro commands and functions. Written in friendly and easy-to-read language, *Writing Excel Macros* will be your quick introduction and guide to writing your own *Excel* macros.

Covers both Macintosh and PC versions of *Excel*.

Acknowledgments

We've said it before, and it's still true: No book gets done in a vacuum. We wish to thank:

Bill Gladstone and the staff of Waterside Productions.
Stephen Levy for patient counsel at the other end of the phone.
Rob Bixby for prudent and careful use of a red pencil.
The Customer Service staff at Microsoft; in particular David Vineberg and Terry Warwick, who went the extra mile on several occasions.
Robert Fry, all-purpose sustainer.
Peter Willis, for help with programming the macros.

Chapter 1
Getting Started with Macros

Introduction

This book is about macro programming in *Excel*, the powerful and flexible spreadsheet from Microsoft. The book is aimed at the businessperson who has had experience with *Excel* spreadsheets, and is interested in learning how to use *Excel's* macro programming capabilities to make his or her work more efficient.

Microsoft has *Excel* versions for the IBM PS/2 Series and IBM PC-AT and clones, and for the Macintosh computers. Since for the most part the program versions operate the same way, this book will address macro programming in both systems. The book covers the features present in *Excel* version 2.01 for the IBM environment and *Excel* version 1.5 for the Macintosh environment.

To run *Excel* in an IBM environment, you need either an IBM PS/2 Series, an IBM PC-AT, a Compaq Deskpro 386, or a computer compatible with one of these models. Your package will include 3½-inch disks and/or 5½-inch disks in a density that works with one of these machines. (Note: *Excel* can't work on an IBM PC-XT unless you have Extended Memory, and even then it works very slowly. It is not recommended that you try to run *Excel* on an IBM PC-XT.)

To run *Excel* version 1.5 in a Macintosh environment, you need a Macintosh 512KE, Macintosh Plus, Macintosh SE, or Macintosh II. Macintosh models with 64K ROMS or less than 512K of RAM cannot run *Excel* 1.5. Your Macintosh must have either a 400K or 800K external disk drive, or a hard disk, or be connected to an AppleShare network. The minimum recommended system configuration must be as follows:

Macintosh Model	Apple System	Finder Version
Macintosh 512KE	3.2	5.3
Macintosh Plus	3.2	5.3
Macintosh SE	4.0	5.4
Macintosh II	4.1	5.5

You can also use *Excel* 1.5 with Apple's MultiFinder operating system. This lets you perform calculations and execute macros as well as save, close, and open documents while working in another application, much the way the IBM version of *Excel* working under *Windows* version 2.0 or higher lets you pass information to other applications while still working with *Excel.*

What's a Macro?

A *macro program* is a set of instructions that runs automatically, once started. It may contain dialog boxes or custom menus that allow a user to choose options, or it may run totally without any keyboard input. It can be anywhere from very short to very long, and it may contain subroutines or references to other macros or files.

Strictly speaking, a macro instruction is a kind of shorthand for a specific sequence of instructions in a particular language. A macro program in *Excel* is similar in many ways to a program written in BASIC, Pascal, C, or some other structured programming language. However, unlike the other programming languages, *Excel's* macro programming instructions work only in a very specific environment—namely, within the spreadsheet program *Excel.*

Macro programs automatically let you handle certain repetitious actions or situations where you want to control carefully what kind of input is allowed. For instance, if you wanted to update the date and time and show these values every time you opened a particular spreadsheet file, you could perform these keyboard actions:

- Enter =NOW( )
- Enter Alt-T, N, then choose the m/d/yy format
- Press the down-arrow key
- Enter =NOW( )
- Enter Alt-T, N, then choose the h:mm AM/PM format

You'd have to do that every time you opened the spreadsheet, unless, of course, you had a macro that would perform these actions automatically every time you opened the file.

Translated to macro instructions, these same steps would look like this:

Timedate
=SELECT("R1C1")
=FORMULA("=NOW( )")
=FORMAT.NUMBER("m/d/yy")
=SELECT("R2C1")
=FORMULA("=NOW( )")
=FORMAT.NUMBER("m/d/yy")
=RETURN( )

Once the spreadsheet file is open, run the macro by opening the file containing the macro, and pressing the designated keys (usually Ctrl and a letter). *Excel* steps through the macro instructions and displays the properly formatted time and date in cells A1 and A2.

Excel has two kinds of macros:
• Command macros
• Function macros

Command Macros

Command macros mimic the actions of *Excel* commands in that they carry out a series of actions that could be performed by worksheet commands, such as specifying commands, entering data, selecting cells, formatting, or selecting parts of a chart. These are particularly useful in situations where there are sets of *Excel* commands that are repeated a number of times.

You can run a command macro either by choosing the Macro Run command, then selecting the name of the macro you want to run, or using a shortcut key such as Ctrl-A. (If you've forgotten the shortcut key for a macro you want to use, choose the Macro Run command and look in the leftmost column. You'll find the letter to use with the Ctrl key in the same row as the macro name.)

Function Macros

Function macros work like *Excel* worksheet functions in that they use values for input, make calculations, and return the resulting values.

You use a function macro where you'd use one or more functions in a worksheet. These are especially useful when you need to do conversions from one number system to another, quickly—such as converting currency from a foreign monetary system to dollars or performing some interim calculation quickly.

To run a function macro, choose the Formula Paste Function command, select the name of the function you want, and then fill in any arguments; or type an equals sign, then the name of the function, followed by arguments enclosed in parentheses.

You can use any of the built-in *Excel* function macros, or you can build your own and store them under a name that lets you use them just as if they came with the program.

Warning: Most function macros require arguments. If you omit an argument, or an argument is improperly stated (remember to separate arguments with commas), *Excel* will warn you, and use the error value #N/A instead of the argument.

Where Do I Use Macros?

Macros save you time and effort. They can perform simple tasks, such as making the text in a cell boldface, or more complex tasks, such as calculating the amount of a given mortgage payment that goes to interest and principle. They can also be helpful in simplifying a large worksheet so others can follow your logic, or so you can reduce calculation time. You can also use them to create menus and dialog boxes on customized application worksheets to help people who don't normally create worksheets enter data and get calculated results. Running under DOS 3.0 in an IBM-AT (or clone) environment, they can even run other applications under *Microsoft Windows* version 2.0 or higher.

You can use a macro when:

- You wind up using the same sequence of steps over and over to perform a calculation involving values that appear in the same row, but different columns.
- You need to check the contents of a cell and determine whether it's a number or text.
- You need to loop through a series of calculations a given number of times, and use only the result.
- You want to set up a spreadsheet so it can be used by others, permitting only certain kinds of values to be entered in response to messages that appear on the screen.

- You have a complex file operation involving getting data from certain other files that are updated independently of the one on which you're working, and incorporating these values into yours. You'd like this to be done automatically so you don't make any mistakes.
- You need to make a status check of files that are updated every day, reporting data from certain equipment. You'd like to set up your equipment so the status check is done every morning at a given time, with the information ready for you when you arrive at work.

Macros, then, are particularly useful in situations where there is repetition of a sequence of steps, where a file will be used by others and you want to protect it against erroneous data entry, or where you want to automate certain actions ranging from the very simple time/date stamping to complicated file access or data evaluation.

General Characteristics of Macros

In *Excel*, macros are created on a *macro sheet*. A macro sheet normally displays formulas, whereas a *worksheet* normally displays values. A macro sheet looks very much like a worksheet, except that the columns are wider:

Figure 1-1. Blank Macro Sheet

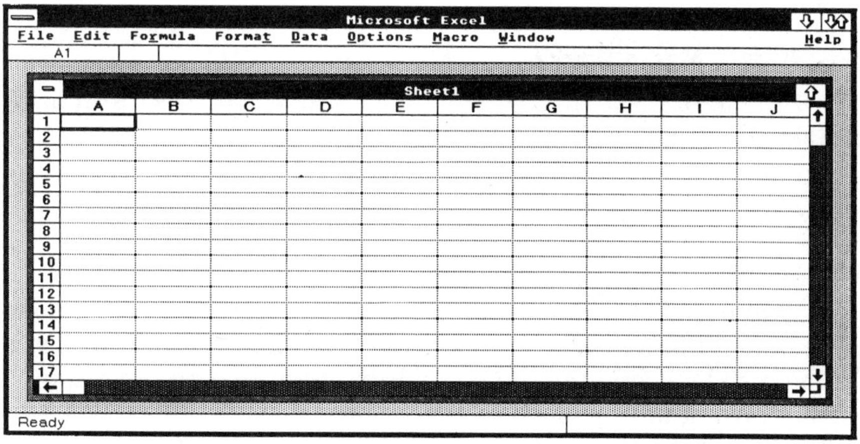

Cell addresses are the same as they would be for a worksheet: The top row is row 1, and the leftmost column is column A, making the top left cell A1. (*Excel* automatically translates the cell addresses into R1C1—row 1 column 1—nomenclature, which you'll see if you use the Recorder.)

Macro instructions are listed on the macro sheet, beginning with row 1. The first cell usually contains the name of the macro, such as INVOICE. The next cell below that contains the first macro instruction. Instructions continue down the column, with the last one being the instruction RETURN, which tells *Excel* that the macro is finished.

The macro may contain references to other sets of macros, such as subroutines or independent macros, each of which begins with its unique name and ends with a =RETURN( ) statement. Several macros can be stored on the same sheet.

If a macro contains comments (as it should), they are placed in the next column to the right of the instructions. Columns can be widened or narrowed the same way spreadsheet columns are adjusted. The contents of each cell remains the same regardless of column width. You can view the contents of the currently active cell in the formula bar.

When you use one of the built-in functions in constructing a macro, you'll see that while there are many macro functions equivalent to worksheet functions, there are also many more functions that work just with macros. If you use the Formula Define Name function in constructing your macro, you'll notice that the dialog box has more options than it does with a worksheet. This is to accommodate different types of macros.

How Does a Macro Work?

On the disk or disks that came with the *Excel* files, Microsoft also provided a number of sample worksheets and macros with the program. If you're running *Excel* on an IBM PC-AT or clone, these samples are in the two libraries EXCELCBT and LIBRARY. If you're running *Excel* on a Macintosh, they're in the folder Sampler Files.

With either version of *Excel* came one or more manuals, and with the manuals came a booklet entitled *Microsoft Excel Sampler*. In the booklet is an example of an application that automates invoicing, using information in an *Excel* database.

In an IBM PC-AT system, the files involved are the template INVTMP.XLS, the supplementary files INVENTRY.XLS and INVOICE.XLS, and the macro file INVOICE.XLM; the example starts on page 66 of the Sampler.

In a Macintosh system, the files involved are the documents INVOICE LIST, INVENTORY, INVOICE TEMPLATE, and IN-VOICE MACROS; the example starts on page 44 of the Sampler.

To get an idea of how macros work, open both the invoice and inventory files (in an IBM environment these are IN-VOICE.XLS and INVENTRY.XLS; in a Macintosh environment these are INVOICE LIST and INVENTORY), and compare what you see on your screen of the Invoice master template file with the examples shown in the booklet. The macro file (IN-VOICE.XLM in the IBM environment; INVOICE MACROS in the Macintosh environment) contains the command macros, each of which performs a different set of actions.

You'll see the names of the macros in bold at the top of the set of instructions, and an explanatory line is on line 2.

The letter in parentheses right after the macro name indicates that the macro has been designed so you can use it with a short-cut key: If you press Ctrl and the letter *V*, the macro will run. Being able to run a macro with a shortcut key is one of the distin-guishing marks of a command macro.

The actual macro instructions start on the third line, where the commands start with an equals sign. These commands are run in logical sequence, ending with the =RETURN( ) command on the last line. Notice that the writer of this macro did some-thing quite commendable: Each instruction is paired with a set of comments in the adjacent column. Comments are highly useful in explaining how a macro works, so another user can decide whether the macro is applicable in a new worksheet.

The first macro is concerned with entering data (M.Invoice in the IBM environment; Enter.Invoice in the Macintosh environ-ment). The second macro (M.Print in IBM; Print.Invoice in Macin-tosh) prints the invoice and clears the template for the next entry.

Interrelated document and macro files work by using an in-ventory template, a list of invoices, and an inventory list as the basic ingredients for the invoicing activities. The invoice macros perform the necessary data shuffling and printing of each invoice.

The blank invoice template, contained in INVTMP.XLS (in IBM) or INVOICE TEMPLATE (in Macintosh), looks like Figure 1-2.

Figure 1-2. Blank Invoice Template

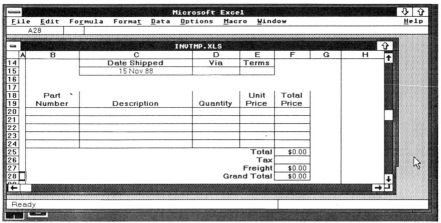

The M.Invoice (or Enter.Invoice) macro is run when you have the template worksheet as the active document, and the invoice, inventory, and macro files open. Choose the Macro Run command, choose the first macro, and press the Enter key to run the macro. Or you can use the shortcut key: Press Ctrl-V. Look at the example in the Sampler to see how your invoice will look after this step.

Next, run the print macro to print the invoice. This macro is listed on the same macro sheet as the data entry macro, under the name M.Print in an IBM environment, or Print.Invoice in a Macintosh environment. To see it, press the PgDn key or scroll down with your mouse.

This macro, like the data entry macro, can be run by using the shortcut key shown. In this case, press Ctrl-P. Once the printing is complete, update the invoice list by running the data entry macro again.

You can construct command macros like these by typing the commands, or you can use Record mode, which turns your keystrokes into macro commands for you. We'll discuss the Recorder in more detail in Chapter 3.

This example shows you how command macros work. The other form of macro is a Function macro. These work much the same way as worksheet functions: You can use the Formula Paste function to paste the general form of the function in place, and then fill in the arguments with your own data. You can also type the function yourself, starting with an equals sign, and enclosing any arguments in parentheses.

Function macros have a particular structure, and because of their complexity may take some study before you feel comfortable writing them.

With a function macro,

1. Specify the type of data you expect as a result of the function macro (the *return value*).
2. Specify an argument function statement for each argument that must be provided when the macro is called.
3. Specify the formulas or actions the macro is to perform.
4. Specify that the macro is to return to the instruction that called it.

Writing macros is like writing programs, and, as such, deserves time and attention to what you want the macro to do, and how to construct the commands logically. Macros can contain branches to other macros, If-Then statements, prompts for user action, application-specific error messages, and a host of other details that emphasize the similarity between macro construction and programming.

Once constructed, however, it's important to do two things to a macro:

- Test and debug it
- Document it

Testing. Testing lets you put the macro through its paces using different values or cell references. You can also try different methods of running it so the logic of the macro gets tested. Most people who write macros recognize that this phase is a bit humbling: You run the macro deliberately looking for errors, and when you find them, you have to debug the macro and fix the logic so it does what you want.

Documenting. A lot of people overlook the documentation phase, thinking that nobody else will need to figure out how the macro works, and that they'll always remember their own logic. Unfortunately, those are the same kind of people who think they'll always remember where they put the car keys, and who wind up missing the first half of a movie trying to find them.

Documenting doesn't necessarily involve writing a book about your macro. Simply include in the second column a brief explanation of the function next to it in the first column.

Adding comments to a macro helps both the writer and anyone else who needs to use the macro understand how it works, and what's needed in the way of arguments or calling sequences.

Comments in *Excel* macros don't interfere with the logic, and take up very little extra memory.

Macro Language Syntax

An *Excel* macro is processed sequentially down a single column of a macro sheet. Instructions within the macro can call other macros by name, and those macros don't necessarily have to be located in the same column as the calling macro.

Figure 1-3 is an example of a simple macro.

Figure 1-3. Sample Macro

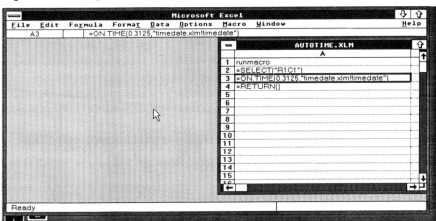

A macro usually starts with the macro's name, which is assigned using the Formula Define Name command. While a name isn't absolutely necessary for a macro, it's a good idea, since a descriptive name lets you know what the macro does. In the example above, we've named the macro *runmacro.*

A macro also has to have a specific endpoint, usually a =RETURN( ) statement. Note that the last instruction in the macro shown above is a =RETURN( ) statement.

Each of the instructions in a macro must begin with an equals sign (=), the same way formulas are stated in *Excel.* It makes sense: Each macro instruction is basically a formula statement to *Excel*, although the language differs from the way formulas are directly stated on a spreadsheet. If an instruction doesn't begin with an equals sign, *Excel* ignores it and continues processing with the next instruction that starts with an equals sign.

There can be more than one macro on a macro sheet. Figure 1-4 is an example of one macro sheet containing three relatively short macros.

Figure 1-4. Three Sample Macros

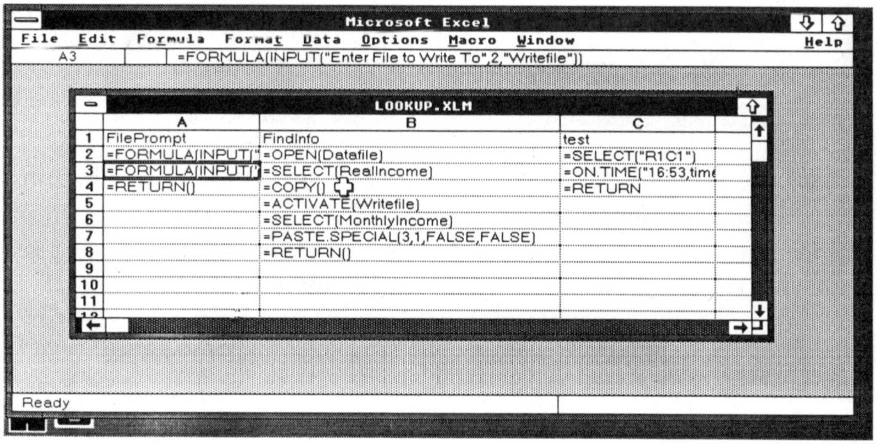

Notice that each has its own name and =RETURN( ) statement. The macro sheet, which is a single file, can be called by the filename. Once the file is identified, you can specify the name of the macro you want to use.

To make your macros more readable, you can make use of the adjacent columns. The column to the left of the instructions can contain names for corresponding macro instructions, much the way you can name values and formulas on a worksheet. The column to the right of the instructions can—and should—contain comments that explain how the macro works. Figure 1-5 shows an example of a macro that's been organized this way.

Figure 1-5. Macro with Name and Comments

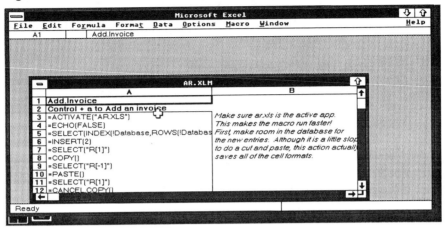

Excel provides a number of built-in commands and functions that work exclusively in the macro environment. We'll explain them in detail in Appendix B. However, as you prepare to write macros, be aware of the fact that macro instructions have to be stated properly, or *Excel* will either give you an error or warning message, or will process your data in a way you probably didn't intend.

Many of *Excel's* command-equivalent instructions are just that: the macro environment equivalent of commands you could execute in a spreadsheet environment. For instance:

Spreadsheet Instruction	Macro Equivalent Instruction
File Open	OPEN
Edit Undo	UNDO
Edit Fill Down	FILL.DOWN
Formula Paste Name	LIST.NAME
Gallery Pie	GALLERY.PIE
Options Set Page Break	SET.PAGE.BREAK

Other macro instructions have no equivalent in the spreadsheet environment:

Macro Instruction	What It Does
FREAD	Reads characters from a text file
FOPEN	Opens a text file *(Continued)*

Macro Instruction	What It Does
INPUT	Displays a dialog box
POKE	Sends data to another application
DOCUMENTS	Returns the name of open documents
DEREF	Returns the value of a cell in a reference
LINKS	Returns the names of all linked documents

Among the more commonly used macro commands are the set of commands that move the active cell. When you move the active cell from location to location on a spreadsheet, you usually use one of the arrow keys, or one of the direction keys (for example, PgUp, PgDn, Home, End). Those keys aren't directly available in a macro, but there are commands that can be used to program active cell movement:

Macro Command	Action
SELECT(*cellref*)	Selects a cell reference: = SELECT(R2C5) moves the active cell to Row 2 Column 5, or E2.
SELECT.END(*number*)	Selects the cell reference in the direction specified by number and moves the active cell there.
SELECT.LAST.CELL	Selects the cell at the end of the document and moves the active cell there

As you proceed through this book, you'll see sample macro programs that use some of these instructions.

The Recorder

One of the easiest ways to grasp just how macro programs work is to use the Recorder. This subprogram included within *Excel* lets you perform some action on your spreadsheet, but transforms the steps you took into a macro program that can then be used again.

You'll soon see an example of how the Recorder works. First, Figure 1-6 shows the spreadsheet you want to create with a macro.

Figure 1-6. Sample Spreadsheet

	A	B	C
1	Time began:		8:55
2	Current time:		15:00
3	Elapsed time:		6:05

This very simple spreadsheet is used to compute elapsed time between a specified time in the past and the current time. We set up this spreadsheet with the following commands:

1. Move the active cell to C1, and select C1 through C3.
2. Choose the Format Number command, and choose the h:mm format.
3. Move the active cell to A1, and type

   Time began:

4. Move the active cell to A2 and type

   Current time:

5. Move the active cell to A3 and type

   Elapsed time:

6. Move the active cell to C1 and type any time. We used 8:55.
7. Move the active cell to C2 and type the formula

   =NOW( )

   Because of the format, this will use the decimal portion of the time/date serial number stored in your computer's memory and display only the hour and minutes of the current time.
8. Move the active cell to C3 and type the formula

   =C2−C1

Your results should match the little spreadsheet shown in Figure 1-6, above. Save the file so you can compare it with the macro you're going to create.

How can you create the same results with a macro? Open a new spreadsheet, and before you type anything else, choose the Macro Recorder command. (In a Macintosh environment, you choose the Macro Record command.) Give the macro a name—we used TIMEDIFF. In the IBM environment, the word *Recording* appears in the status bar at the bottom of the screen; the word doesn't appear in a Macintosh environment.

Now repeat the steps above. Your steps will be translated by the Recorder into macro instructions. When you complete the steps, choose the Stop Recorder command. This allows *Excel* to mark an end to the macro actions.

Use the Window menu to choose the Macro1 window (this is the temporary filename *Excel* has given the macro). You'll see a list of macro instructions that look like this:

14

Figure 1-7. Sample Spreadsheet as a Macro in IBM Environment

	A
1	timediff
2	=SELECT("R1C3:R3C3")
3	=FORMAT.NUMBER("h:mm")
4	=SELECT("R1C1")
5	=FORMULA("Time began:")
6	=SELECT("R2C1")
7	=FORMULA("Current time:")
8	=SELECT("R3C1")
9	=FORMULA("Elapsed time:")
10	=SELECT("R1C3")
11	=FORMULA("8:55:00 AM")
12	=SELECT("R2C3")
13	=FORMULA("=NOW()")
14	=SELECT("R3C3")
15	=FORMULA("=R[-1]C-R[-2]C")
16	=RETURN()

Save the macro as a macro file. You can use the same file-name; *Excel* will append the extension .XLM to identify it as a macro file.

There are some interesting things to note about the instructions *Excel* used as translations of your actions:

- Each time you move the active cell to a new location, you are invoking a SELECT macro instruction.
- *Excel* uses the R1C1 form of cell references, rather than the A1 form. It doesn't matter if you type cell references in A1 form— when stored as macro instructions, *Excel* translates them all to R1C1 form.
- Arguments enclosed in the parentheses after the macro instruction are usually also enclosed in double quotes. Note the way *Excel* stored the time format after the FORMAT.NUMBER instruction, and the way the cell references are stated after a SELECT instruction.

To see how the macro works, open a new, blank spreadsheet and choose the Macro Run command, then specify the macro file-name you used. The macro runs automatically, creating the same spreadsheet you saw in Figure 1-6.

Some Sample Macros

This section contains some relatively simple macros you can copy and try out for yourself. We'll demonstrate some of the techniques you can use with your own macros.

15

Time/Date Stamping

This little macro lets you put the current time and date in cells A1 and A2 of your spreadsheet. It uses the =NOW( ) function to get your computer's time/date serial number, and displays it in one of the date and time formats.

We named the macro TIMEDATE, but you could name it something else. To run it, open a spreadsheet, open the macro file containing TIMEDATE, choose the Macro Run command, and select the TIMEDATE macro. The resulting date and time will appear on your spreadsheet.

The macro instructions are listed in Figures 1-8 and 1-9.

Figure 1-8. TIMEDATE Macro, IBM Environment

	A
1	timedate
2	=SELECT("R1C1")
3	=FORMAT.NUMBER("m/d/yy")
4	=FORMULA("=NOW()")
5	=SELECT("R2C1")
6	=FORMAT.NUMBER("h:mm AM/PM")
7	=FORMULA("=NOW()")
8	=RETURN()

Figure 1-9. TIMEDATE Macro, Macintosh Environment

	A
1	timedate
2	=SELECT("R1C1")
3	=FORMAT.NUMBER("m/d/yy")
4	=FORMULA("=NOW()")
5	=SELECT("r2c1")
6	=FORMAT.NUMBER("h:mm AM/PM")
7	=FORMULA("=NOW()")
8	=RETURN()

As the macro appears above, the date appears in the m/d/yy format and the time appears in the h:mm format. If you want to use another format, edit the macro instructions that start =FORMAT.NUMBER to reflect the format you want.

As stated above, the macro also puts the date in cell A1 and the time in A2. If you want to use another location, such as G1 and G2, or A1 and B1, edit the =SELECT( ) macro instructions to reflect (in R1C1 style) the locations you want to use.

Run a Program at a Specified Time

Wouldn't it be nice if you could set up your computer so it would run one or more programs for you automatically, and have the results ready and waiting for you when you arrive at work?

Here's a simple macro for the IBM environment that uses a macro instruction (ON.TIME) which lets you do just that: It happens to be set up so it will run another program every day at 7:30 a.m. (Because *Excel* 1.5 for the Macintosh doesn't include the ON.TIME macro instruction, this macro won't work in that environment.)

Figure 1-10. Automatic Clock Macro

	A
1	runmacro
2	=SELECT("R1C1")
3	=ON.TIME(0.3125,"timedate.xlm!timedate")
4	=RETURN()

A macro like this requires the computer either to be left on all night, or that there be some automatic mechanism that turns on the computer and uses an AUTOEXEC.BAT file to load *Excel* and the requisite macro files. When setting up such a mechanism, be sure the final step leaves a blank spreadsheet on the screen.

In this case, at 7:30 a.m. each day, this program automatically runs the TIMEDATE shown above.

Notice that, other than the title and the =RETURN( ) statement, this macro contains only two instructions. One, the SELECT instruction, positions the active cell (in this case, cell A1). The other, the ON.TIME instruction, specifies the time the macro is to run (in this case, 0.3125 is the serial number for 7:30 a.m.) and the filename and macro name of the macro program to be run (here, the filename is TIMEDATE.XLM, and the macro name happens to be TIMEDATE).

You can change this macro to perform what you want done:

- Repeat the SELECT and ON.TIME instructions for each macro program you want to run. Be sure to stagger the serial time number specified in the ON.TIME instruction so each macro you want can be run in sequence. You don't want all your programs to run at 7:30 a.m., for instance—only the first will be run at that time, then the next will wait for the next time 7:30 a.m. rolls around.
- Change the cell reference used in the SELECT instruction so the running of each program doesn't overlay the previous program's display.
- Use different macros, on different files if you need to. Each filename and macro name must be stated as text (enclosed in double quotes), and each filename used must be an open file.

Stock Portfolio

This little spreadsheet can help you update your stock portfolio and track the annual yield on what you hold. It requires that you set up the spreadsheet headings and formats beforehand, then run the macro for each stock you own.

Figure 1-11 is an example of the way the spreadsheet should look when you're finished.

Figure 1-11. Stock Portfolio Spreadsheet

	A	B	C	D	E	F	G
1	Stock Portfolio						
2	Stock prices	18-Nov-88					
3				Share		Share	
4		Date bought	#Shares	Pur. price	Cum. Div.	Cur. Price	Ann. Yield
5	Amalgamated General	4-Feb-87	500	21.625	25	47	0.65791522
6	Wholly Cereal	19-May-87	200	43.5	104	52.5	0.14146326
7	Water Resources	20-May-87	1000	52.75	1040	49.75	-0.0372248
8	Northern Financial	20-Oct-87	500	16.875	310	25.375	0.4677538
9	Shoes Inc.	15-Dec-87	300	12.25	225	21	0.77430905

You could construct the entire spreadsheet with the Recorder turned on, but when you finish, you'd have a macro program that typed the same stocks, number of shares, closing and current prices, and cumulative dividends every time it ran, in addition to calculating the annual yield. That doesn't make sense in the long run, but it makes sense to do it that way the first time you construct the stock portfolio. Figure 1-12 shows a macro that simply constructs the portfolio, with no facility to change values or enter new stocks.

Figure 1-12 is a macro constructed with the Recorder the first time we set up the portfolio spreadsheet. You can use it to format the spreadsheet, and to construct the yield formula in Column G. Change the names, dates, prices, and dividends to reflect stocks you're interested in.

In the long run, however, you want a macro that will let you enter data for a new stock each time you use the portfolio spreadsheet, and calculate the annual yield based on the data entered. To do that, you need to have the macro prompt you for data, allow you to enter it in the proper places, then calculate the yield, and finally let you decide whether you're finished or have more to enter.

Figure 1-12. The Recorded Stock Portfolio Macro

	A
1	stockmac
2	=FORMULA("Stock Portfolio")
3	=SELECT("R2C1")
4	=FORMULA("Stock prices")
5	=SELECT("R2C1")
6	=COLUMN.WIDTH(20)
7	=SELECT("R2C2")
8	=COLUMN.WIDTH(12)
9	=FORMAT.NUMBER("d-mmm-yy")
10	=FORMULA("=NOW()")
11	=SELECT("R4C2")
12	=FORMULA("Date bought")
13	=SELECT("R5C2:R9C2")
14	=FORMAT.NUMBER("d-mmm-yy")
15	=SELECT("R4C3")
16	=FORMULA("#Shares")
17	=SELECT("R3C4")
18	=FORMULA("Share")
19	=SELECT("R4C4")
20	=FORMULA("Pur. price")
21	=SELECT("R4C5")
22	=FORMULA("Cum. Div.")
23	=SELECT("R3C6")
24	=FORMULA("Share")
25	=SELECT("R4C6")
26	=FORMULA("Cur. Price")
27	=SELECT("R4C7")
28	=FORMULA("Ann. Yield")
29	=SELECT("R5C1")
30	=FORMULA("Amalgamated General")
31	=SELECT("R6C1")
32	=FORMULA("Wholly Cereal")
33	=SELECT("R7C1")
34	=FORMULA("Water Resources")
35	=SELECT("R8C1")
36	=FORMULA("Northern Financial")
37	=SELECT("R9C1")
38	=FORMULA("Shoes Inc.")
39	=SELECT("R5C2")
40	=FORMULA("2/4/1987")
41	=SELECT("R5C3")
42	=FORMULA("500")
43	=SELECT("R5C4")
44	=FORMULA("21.625")
45	=SELECT("R5C5")
46	=FORMULA("=0.05*RC[-2]")
47	=SELECT("R5C6")
48	=FORMULA("47")
49	=SELECT("R5C7")
50	=FORMULA("=(((RC[-4]*RC[-1])-(RC[-4]*RC[-3])+RC[-1])/(RC[-4]*RC[-3]))/((R2C2-RC[-5])/365)")
51	=SELECT("R6C2")
52	=FORMULA("5/19/1987")
53	=SELECT("R6C3")
54	=FORMULA("200")
55	=SELECT("R6C4")
56	=FORMULA("43.5")
57	=SELECT("R6C5")
58	=FORMULA("0.52*C6")
59	=SELECT("R6C6")
60	=FORMULA("52.5")
61	=SELECT("R5C7")
62	=COPY()
63	=SELECT("R6C7")
64	=PASTE()
65	=CANCEL.COPY()
66	=SELECT("R6C5")

Figure 1-12. The Recorded Stock Portfolio Macro (Continued)

	A
67	=FORMULA("=0.52*RC[-2]")
68	=SELECT("R7C2")
69	=FORMULA("5/20/1987")
70	=SELECT("R7C3")
71	=FORMULA("1000")
72	=SELECT("R7C4")
73	=FORMULA("52.75")
74	=SELECT("R7C5")
75	=FORMULA("=1.04*RC[-2]")
76	=SELECT("R7C6")
77	=FORMULA("49.75")
78	=SELECT("R6C7")
79	=COPY()
80	=SELECT("R7C7")
81	=PASTE()
82	=CANCEL.COPY()
83	=SELECT("R8C2")
84	=FORMULA("10/20/1987")
85	=SELECT("R8C3")
86	=FORMULA("500")
87	=SELECT("R8C4")
88	=FORMULA("16.875")
89	=SELECT("R8C5")
90	=FORMULA("=0.62*RC[-2]")
91	=SELECT("R8C6")
92	=FORMULA("25.375")
93	=SELECT("R7C7")
94	=COPY()
95	=SELECT("R8C7")
96	=PASTE()
97	=CANCEL.COPY()
98	=SELECT("R9C2")
99	=FORMULA("12/15/1987")
100	=SELECT("R9C3")
101	=FORMULA("300")
102	=SELECT("R9C4")
103	=FORMULA("12.25")
104	=SELECT("R9C5")
105	=FORMULA("=0.75*RC[-2]")
106	=SELECT("R9C6")
107	=FORMULA("21")
108	=SELECT("R8C7")
109	=COPY()
110	=SELECT("R9C7")
111	=PASTE()
112	=CANCEL.COPY()
113	=RETURN()

Figure 1-13 shows the macro that will let you do that.

When run, adding a new stock acquisition for the company Newstock, the spreadsheet looks like Figure 1-14. (Note that some of the cells have been specially formatted to reflect dollar amounts. Note also that these macros should open the spreadsheet on which they act. In order to do this they should have this instruction in the first line of the macro: =ACTIVATE ("FILENAME.XL?") where *FILENAME.XL?* is the name of the file the macro opens and writes to. In preparing to run this macro, you should also define the variables used in the spreadsheet FILENAME.XL?.)

Figure 1-13. Stock Portfolio Macro

	A	B
1		stocktem
2	Start	=SELECT("R[+1]C1")
3		=FORMULA(INPUT("Please enter the stock name",2,"Prompt"))
4		=SELECT("R[+0]C[+1]")
5		=FORMAT.NUMBER("d-mmm-yy")
6		=FORMULA(INPUT("Enter the date bought",1,"Prompt"))
7		=SELECT("R[+0]C[+1]")
8		=FORMULA(INPUT("Enter number of shares bought",1,"Prompt"))
9		=SELECT("R[+0]C[+1]")
10		=FORMULA(INPUT("Enter purchase price per share",1,"Prompt"))
11		=SELECT("R[+0]C[+1]")
12		=FORMULA(INPUT("Enter amt. of dividends to date",1,"Prompt"))
13		=SELECT("R[+0]C[+1]")
14		=FORMULA(INPUT("Enter current price per share",1,"Prompt"))
15		=SELECT("R[-1]C[+1]")
16		=COPY()
17		=SELECT("R[+1]C[+0]")
18		=PASTE()
19		=CANCEL.COPY()
20		=SELECT("R[+0]C[+1]")
21		=FORMULA(INPUT("Do you want to enter another stock?(y/n)",2,"Prompt"))
22		=IF(ACTIVE.CELL()="y",GOTO(Again),GOTO(End))
23	Again	=CLEAR()
24		=GOTO(Start)
25	End	=CLEAR()
26		=RETURN()

Figure 1-14. Stock Portfolio After Running Macro

	A	B	C	D	E	F	G
1	Stock portfolio						
2	Stock prices	3-Nov-88					
3				Share		Share	
4		Date bought	# Shares	Pur. Price	Cum. Div.	Cur. Price	Ann. Yield
5	Amalgamated General	4-Feb-87	500	21.63	25.00	47.00	0.67
6	Wholly Cereal	19-May-87	200	43.50	104.00	52.50	0.15
7	Water Resources	20-May-87	1000	52.75	1040.00	49.75	-0.03
8	Northern Financial	20-Oct-87	500	16.88	310.00	25.38	0.52
9	Shoes Inc.	15-Dec-87	300	12.25	225.00	21.00	0.87
10	Newstock	1-Sep-88	100	14.75	0	14.75	0.00

Note that this macro must be run on an existing worksheet set up like the one shown in Figure 1-13, complete with the formula in Column G. It differs from the command macros shown up to this point because its use of INPUT statements allow proper entry of new data (lines 3, 6, 8, 10, 12, 14, and 21), and the IF statement lets you specify whether you're finished.

There are a few other differences, too. The references in the SELECT statements are relative to the current position of the active cell (for example, =SELECT("R[−1]C[+1]"), which means one less row and one more column). Several of the instructions have been named *(Start, Again,* and *End)* so the GOTO instructions in lines 22 and 24 will work.

Summary

This chapter has shown you some basic concepts about using macros in *Excel,* and given you several examples of how macros could be used in business situations. The next chapters in this book will look at macros in more detail. Chapter 2 will show you how to create a macro, Chapter 3 shows you how to use the Recorder, Chapter 4 discusses handing data and variables, Chapter 5 is a brief introduction to programming concepts in general, Chapter 6 discusses how to work with other files, Chapter 7 shows you how to debug and edit your macros, and Chapter 8 looks at some advanced topics, such as creating automatic macros and using customizing techniques. Appendix A contains a quick reference guide to the macro commands and functions, and Appendix B contains a more detailed look at the syntax and use of each macro function.

Chapter 2
Creating a Macro

There are two ways to create a macro in *Excel:*

- Type all the macro commands and operations into a blank macro worksheet, define the macro range, and optionally assign a single-key identifier.
- Use the Recorder to transcribe your steps as you construct a worksheet that accomplishes what you want; then after you've turned off the Recorder, edit it if necessary, define it as a macro, and optionally assign a key.

While the Recorder is frequently a simpler way of creating a set of macro commands, it also records every mistake and correction you make in the process. Sometimes it's easier to think through what you want to do first, then write the commands, and finally go through the steps necessary to declare the commands a working macro.

This chapter will show you how to create macros both ways, but will concentrate on the organization and editing of a macro. You'll see how to sketch what you want the macro to do, how to use the Recorder and what to do with a macro freshly created by the Recorder, where to use macro functions, and how to set up your macro so it can handle various kinds of errors. Some naming conventions will be discussed, as well as how to handle documentation, and how to execute your macro.

Sketching What You Want to Accomplish

Form follows function. That's an oft-repeated design maxim that applies to macros as well as to skyscrapers. What you want your macro to do should dictate how it looks. If you want your macro to step straight through a series of commands and exit, you can use a linear organization (Figure 2-1).

Figure 2-1. Linear Macro Organization

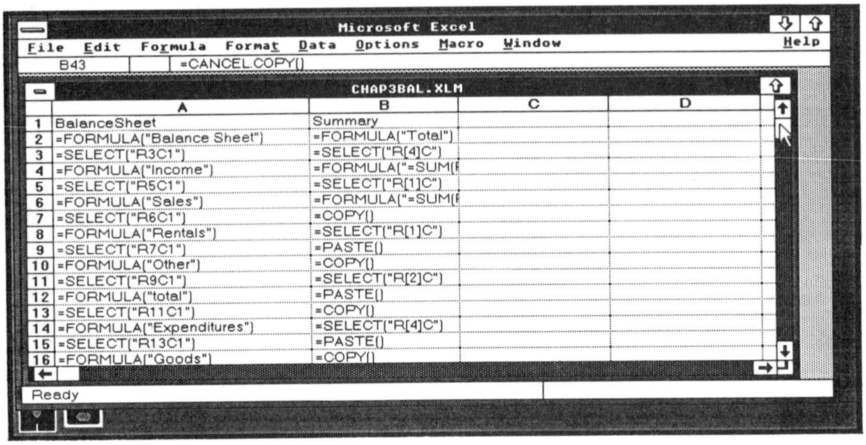

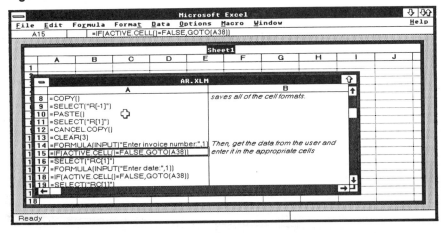

On the other hand, if you want your macro to test for a condition, and take either of two paths depending on the result it finds, it might look somewhat like Figure 2-2.

Figure 2-2. Macro with Conditional Test

Here's another case: You may want a macro that loops through a series of steps a specified number of times, perhaps each time writing or calculating data in a new column each time, and then going on to other steps. It would look something like Figure 2-3.

Figure 2-3. Macro with Loop

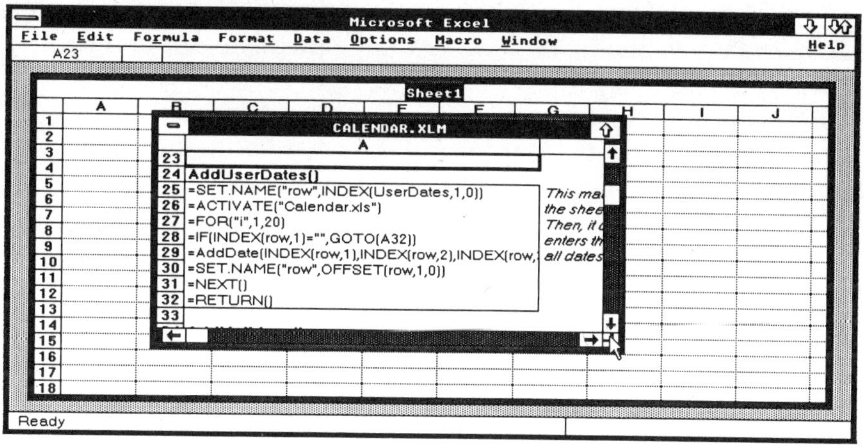

And here's yet another case: Your macro needs to use a short little macro that's already been written. Why incorporate that code into your macro when you can branch to it with one call, and come right back when its actions are finished? Figure 2-4 shows how that would look.

How do you know which form your macro will take? It's not all that complex. Start with what you want your macro to do.

Is the purpose of your macro to print something? Is it to copy data from one place to another? Is it to perform some calculation? If possible, it's best to limit the number of things your macro is

Figure 2-4. Macro with Subroutine Call

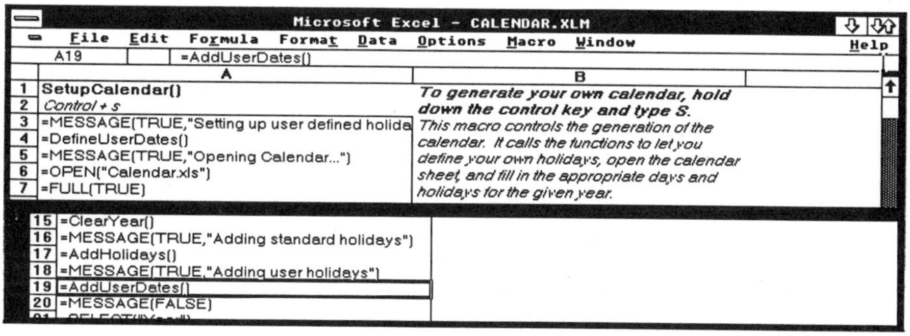

going to do: Keep it simple. You can always use several macros to perform a complete operation of fetching data and doing calculations, arranging the data in one or more spreadsheets, and printing out the data.

As you start thinking about your macro, sketch it out on a piece of paper. State the purpose of the macro at the top to remind you when you get distracted later on by some of the possibilities.

Are there some things that need to happen before your macro fetches data? Does it need to format certain cells or change the width of columns or height of rows? Does it need to clear existing data from some of the cells? List the things that need to happen before your macro starts working with data.

Next, where does your macro get the data it's going to use? Is that data going to be the same every time, or will it change, depending on other conditions? Are there some conditions where you don't want to use the data (such as if a cell contains error values like #NA or #ERROR)? Where does it put any new data it calculates? List where the data is coming from, and how it needs to be tested.

How many different ways can you identify that things could go wrong while your macro is processing data? One was mentioned in the previous paragraph: What will your macro do if it encounters an error value in a cell, rather than numeric or text data? There might be other situations: If your macro encounters

Figure 2-5. Flowcharting Symbols

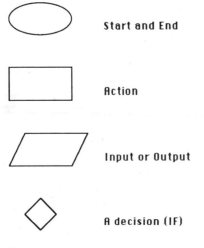

Start and End

Action

Input or Output

A decision (IF)

text data in a situation where it's supposed to perform a numeric calculation, what should it do? What happens if the cell is blank? What happens if a decimal is in the wrong place? What if the wrong format has been used?

These are more testing situations. However, you may have already dealt with this issue in another part of your work, and hence can assume that incoming data is in the form you need. Be sure you've covered all the bases before your macro finishes.

Note: It's perfectly acceptable to have your macro quit early if it encounters the wrong data. Just be sure that the person running the macro gets some sort of notification, either a system error message, or a message the macro causes to be displayed.

Now, about the actions your macro will take: What's the result of your macro's work? Is it going to print something? Is it going to return some values? How will you know when your macro has done its work?

Once you've identified these key sets of actions and set up a kind of game plan, you can use flow chart symbols to translate the comments to a logical flow. You probably won't need more than the symbols shown in Figure 2-5.

Translate your comments to a flowchart. It may look like this:

Figure 2-6. Sample Flowchart

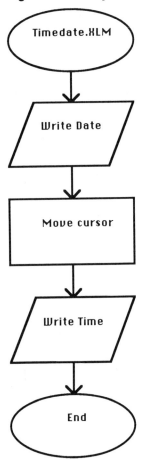

Follow some simple rules for translating your ideas to a flow-chart:

- Don't use any step more than one time. If you find you need to use a step more than once, think about how you can create a loop or subroutine so it only gets written once, but used whenever you need it.
- Make sure each step connects to the previous one and the next one.
- Don't let connecting lines cross each other.

- Simplify, simplify, simplify. If a process starts to look too complex, think about breaking it out as a separate macro, one you can call from a main macro.
- Give each macro one entrance point and one exit point.

Once you've decided how your macro is going to work, you'll have a better idea of where you'll need a command macro, and where you'll need a function macro. These terms were defined briefly in Chapter 1, but to reiterate the differences:

- A command macro is used to perform actions, which can include calculations. Command macros can involve the opening and closing of a file, printing a document, various movement around a window, formatting operations, selecting a cell or range, naming a cell or range, or using one of *Excel's* predefined functions. You run a command macro either by typing its name in a cell, choosing it when you specify the Macro Run command, or pressing the shortcut key.
- A function macro is used to perform a calculation and return a value. Its form requires that you begin with an ARGUMENT statement that describes its input, use that input in a formula or series of formulas, then return the value in a specified location. You run a function macro only by choosing its name on the Macro Run menu or using the shortcut key.

If you just need a macro that steps through one or more formulas, you'll be writing a function macro. If you want your macro to do anything else, you'll be writing a command macro.

One last task in sketching your macro: Decide on a name, and decide whether you'll want to be able to call it using a shortcut key. Remember that your macro can be grouped with other macros on a single macro file, but that its name must differ from others. Its shortcut key must also be different from those used with any others on an open macro file.

You may wind up with a set of notes looking something like Figure 2-7.

Figure 2-7. Sketch of a Macro

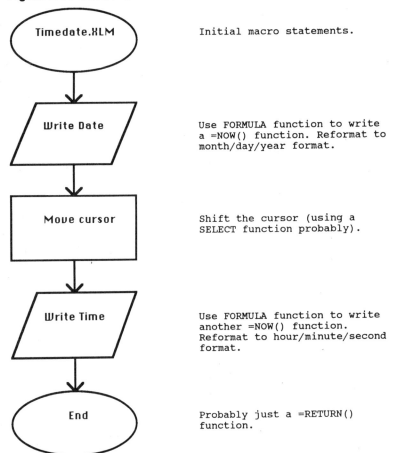

Timedate.XLM — Initial macro statements.

Write Date — Use FORMULA function to write a =NOW() function. Reformat to month/day/year format.

Move cursor — Shift the cursor (using a SELECT function probably).

Write Time — Use FORMULA function to write another =NOW() function. Reformat to hour/minute/second format.

End — Probably just a =RETURN() function.

Using the Recorder

The Recorder will be discussed in much more depth in the next chapter, but it's worth a quick overview here. The Recorder basically translates your keystrokes on a worksheet into macro commands. You turn it on and off with one of the commands on the Macro menu.

When you turn on the Recorder, you're prompted for a name for the macro you're about to create. *Excel* suggests a name and a shortcut key. If it's the first macro opened during the current session, the suggested name will be *Record1* and the shortcut key will be *A*.

Once you've assigned a name and (optionally) chosen a shortcut key, you're free to move around your spreadsheet. Every keystroke will be recorded and translated into macro commands, including all your mistakes and corrections. Don't worry about making mistakes. The beauty of using the Recorder is that you can later edit your mistakes, cleaning up the logic and perhaps streamlining what you've done.

It's highly likely that the first few times you use the Recorder you'll get some good ideas about how to make the macro more efficient after you see how the Recorder translated your steps into macro commands. Seeing your keystrokes as macro commands will probably give you some further ideas about grouping commands and using ranges.

For instance, Figure 2-8 is a small spreadsheet example.

Figure 2-8. Sample Spreadsheet

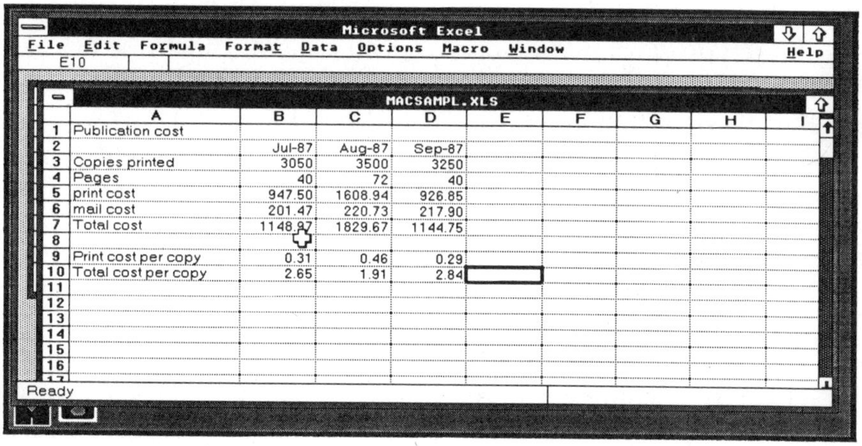

And Figure 2-9 shows how the Recorder translated it.

That's a lot of instructions to create a little spreadsheet only four columns wide by ten rows deep. Further, if you look closely at the macro instructions, you'll see that the macro puts all the data in, as well as all the formats and formulas. In a general-purpose macro, you'd want to put in our own data once the macro had set up the labels, formats, and formulas. What can be done to this macro to make it more general and more efficient?

First, notice how *Excel* has translated your movement of the active cell into macro commands. Each of these locations follows the macro command =SELECT. The information in the parenthe-

Figure 2-9. Sample Spreadsheet as Recorded

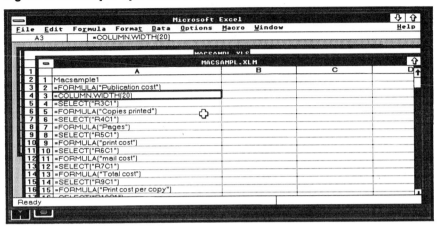

ses is the equivalent R1C1 cell address where you moved the active cell as you were moving through the spreadsheet.

Since you started the worksheet on a blank sheet, the active cell was already at R1C1 (cell A1), so it didn't need a =SELECT statement when you typed the label *Publication cost*. However, when you moved to A3 to type *Copies printed*, you selected a cell; hence the statement in line 4: =SELECT("R3C1").

If you scan down the list of macro instructions, you'll see that almost every other instruction is a =SELECT statement. Each of these involves positioning the active cell. As you might guess, the SELECT statement is very common in macros. When you edit the macro, you can take out some of these statements, depending on what else is going on there.

The next step is to identify the data's location. These are cells where you've entered text or numbers. Some of those you want to keep, and some you'd like to either modify or remove.

Notice that each of these is in a cell where the macro statement starts with =FORMULA. The FORMULA command indicates that what follows is either text or numeric data or formulas, and is another very common macro statement.

The purpose in having the macro available at all, instead of simply saving the whole thing as a worksheet file, is to be able to enter different data when you need to, but use the same headings, formats, and formulas. It would be somewhat inconvenient to write over existing data, and would be more convenient if the macro could create a template so each time you entered data, you'd get a new worksheet.

The first targets for elimination are those cells where you entered numeric data. Looking at the sample worksheet, you can see that there are numbers in the range B3 to D10. However, some of those numbers are computed by the worksheet, and some are numbers you entered. The numbers you entered are in B3 through D6, and on the macro sheet will be identified as R3C2 through R6C4.

Figure 2-10 shows an example of the sort of thing you're looking for.

Figure 2-10. Macro Instructions, Data

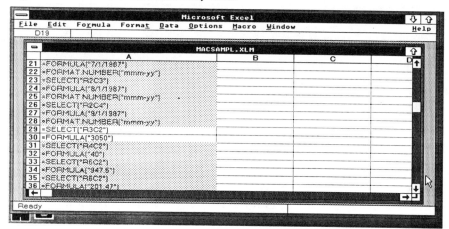

The macro instruction on line 29 selects cell B3, and the instruction on line 30 inserts the value 3050 into the cell. The value 3050 was accurate for the worksheet you created, but in the general application, you want to enter your own data here. Lines 29 and 30 are good candidates for deletion.

Lines 31 through 36 are also good candidates. In each case, the macro has selected a cell, and inserted data.

However, lines 37 and 38 are another story.

Cell B7 contains a formula that sums the two costs above it. The positioning of the active cell is done in the SELECT statement on line 37, and the formula is in line 38.

Figure 2-11. Macro Instructions, Formula

	A	B	C	D
					=SELECT("R3C2")
21	=FORMULA("7/1/1987")			
22	=FORMAT.NUMBER("mmm-yy")			
23	=SELECT("R2C3")			
24	=FORMULA("8/1/1987")			
25	=FORMAT.NUMBER("mmm-yy")			
26	=SELECT("R2C4")			
27	=FORMULA("9/1/1987")			
28	=FORMAT.NUMBER("mmm-yy")			
29	=SELECT("R3C2")			
30	=FORMULA("3050")			
31	=SELECT("R4C2")			
32	=FORMULA("40")			
33	=SELECT("R5C2")			
34	=FORMULA("947.5")			
35	=SELECT("R6C2")			
36	=FORMULA("201.47")			
37	=SELECT("R7C2")			
38	=FORMULA("=R[-2]C+R[-1]C")			
39	=SELECT("R9C2")			
40	=FORMULA("=R[-4]C/R[-6]C")			

Notice that the formula doesn't refer directly to B5 and B6; rather, it uses the relative form of reference. The formula

$$= R[-2]C + R[-1]C$$

means, literally, *take the value in the cell two rows up in the current column, and add to it the value in the cell one row up in the current column.* This means that whatever is placed two rows up will be added to whatever is placed one row up, and the result stored in the currently active cell. As long as the formula represents the situation you want, you'll want to keep this formula in the final edited version of the macro.

Now look at the formulas determining the cost per copy. They're in lines 39 through 42, and affect cells B9 and B10.

These formulas, as with the formula in line 38, involve placement of the active cell, then construction of the formula using relative cell references. In the case of print cost per copy, the formula in column B divides the print cost (in B5) by the number of copies printed (in B3). In the case of total cost per copy, the formula divides the total cost (in B7) by the number of copies printed. The formulas in rows 7, 9, and 10 are ones you want to keep.

Next, the formulas in B7, B9, and B10 are copied in the two columns to the right. These you want to keep, as well.

Figure 2-12. Macro Instructions, Formulas with Relative References

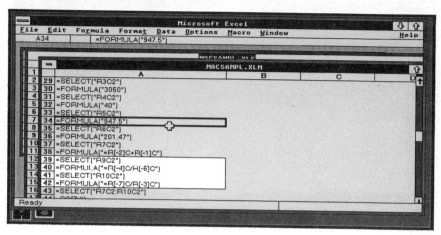

The instruction in line 43 selects the range to be copied. The instruction in line 45 selects where the source cells are to be placed. Notice that there must be a matching CANCEL.COPY( ) macro instruction when a COPY( ) macro instruction is used.

Another set of labels you want to consider saving are the column headings in row 1. These were set up in the macro instructions in lines 20 through 28.

Figure 2-13. Macro Instruction for Copying

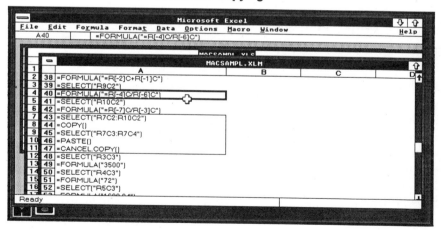

Figure 2-14. Sample Date Macro Instructions

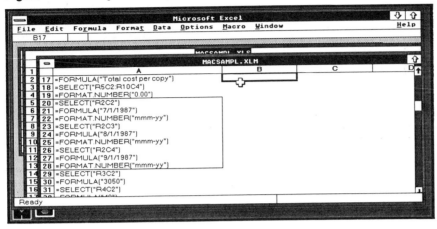

However, that's a pretty inefficient way to handle dates. Wouldn't it be better to select all the cells in row 2 that you're likely to need, and format them before entering any data? That way, the column label could be entered in any acceptable form, and would be displayed in the format you chose. (In fact, the column label on the spreadsheet was actually typed as *Jul-87* and was translated by *Excel* so the macro instruction carries it as *7/1/1987*.)

The instructions to do that, in this case (assuming you want no more than three columns, and the date will be in row 2, as shown), are as follows:

=SELECT("R2C2:R2C5")
=FORMAT.NUMBER("mmm-yy")

That's much more efficient. Using these two instructions, when the next user enters the date in any date form in one of these three cells, it will appear as you want it.

One more item: What number formats do you want? The instructions on lines 18 and 19 format the range B5 through D10 as decimal:

Figure 2-15. Macro Instructions, Number Format

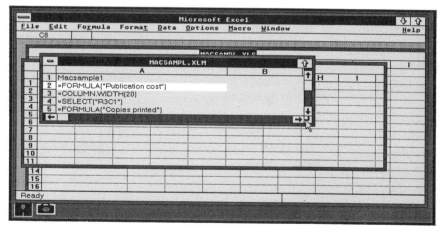

(Note that you've purposely left B3 through D4 unformatted; the numbers entered here are integers. If you want to protect against entry mistakes, you may want to insert some macro instructions that make this range into integer format.)

Keep the number format instructions in the edited form of the macro.

Last item: Note that the column width was changed in line 2 in Figure 2-16.

Figure 2-16. Macro Instruction. Column Width

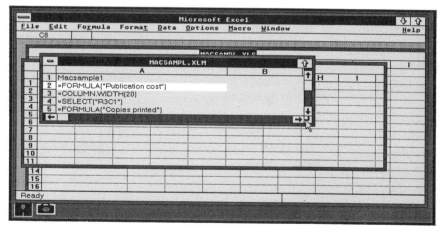

As the title was typed in cell A1, you may have noted that you were going over the cell's right border. That's why the =COLUMN.WIDTH instruction came after the =FORMULA instruction. A width of 20 characters would probably be adequate for any row labels needed. Keep this instruction, too.

Finally, what about all the data you entered, as reflected in the instructions in lines 48 through 63? (You need to keep the =RETURN instruction in order to make this a proper macro.)

Figure 2-17. Macro Instructions, Data

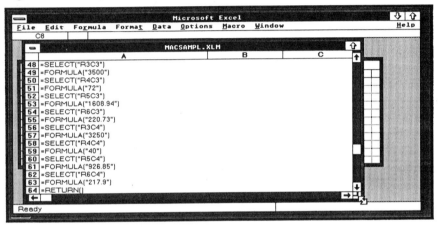

Each pair of =SELECT and =FORMULA instructions puts data in a specific cell. You don't want the macro to do that. You want to be able insert data after the macro has run and set up the template. Now you can delete all of these lines.

Now that you've decided what to keep and what to delete, you can use *Excel's* Edit menu to remove the instructions you don't want. To do that, simply move the active cell to the first line of a range you want to delete, extend the range so the two or more cells involved are highlighted, and choose the Edit Delete command.

When you're finished editing, your macro should look like this:

Figure 2-18. Edited Sample Macro

	A
1	Macsample1
2	=FORMULA("Publication cost")
3	=COLUMN.WIDTH(20)
4	=SELECT("R3C1")
5	=FORMULA("Copies printed")
6	=SELECT("R4C1")
7	=FORMULA("Pages")
8	=SELECT("R5C1")
9	=FORMULA("print cost")
10	=SELECT("R6C1")
11	=FORMULA("mail cost")
12	=SELECT("R7C1")
13	=FORMULA("Total cost")
14	=SELECT("R9C1")
15	=FORMULA("Print cost per copy")
16	=SELECT("R10C1")
17	=FORMULA("Total cost per copy")
18	=SELECT("R5C2:R10C4")
19	=FORMAT.NUMBER("0.00")
20	=SELECT("R2C2:R2C5")
21	=FORMAT.NUMBER("mmm-yy")
22	=SELECT("R7C2")
23	=FORMULA("=R[-2]C+R[-1]C")
24	=SELECT("R9C2")
25	=FORMULA("=R[-4]C/R[-6]C")
26	=SELECT("R10C2")
27	=FORMULA("=R[-7]C/R[-3]C")
28	=SELECT("R7C2:R10C2")
29	=COPY()
30	=SELECT("R7C3:R7C4")
31	=PASTE()
32	=CANCEL.COPY()
33	=RETURN()

The process you've just stepped through shows the value of the Recorder in translating keystrokes to macro instructions, and also the necessity for editing the macro created by the Recorder so your final version is more general-purpose.

Macro Structure

There are two elements of structure that need discussing in this section:

- Structure of the macro sheet
- Structure of the macro's logic

There is no one legal way to structure a macro sheet in *Excel*. The only rules are that a macro command must begin with an equals sign (=), the syntax of the individual command must be followed, the title of the macro is in the first line, and macro commands are processed sequentially down a column. Other than those four items, you can place a macro anywhere on a macro sheet.

However, there are a few conventions that will probably help you (or others) recognize how your macro works, and that's what you refer to as *structure* of the macro sheet.

Names are an important part of any macro that's more than just a few lines long. If, for instance, you have a conditional situation where the macro tests for the presence or absence of some value, the program logic has to offer at least two options: Path A is where the program goes if the value is where you tested, and Path B is where it goes otherwise. But how do you identify Path A? How do you identify Path B?

When you name the start of Path A and the start of Path B, you're telling *Excel* that these are pointers that can be used to identify particular instructions, just as you probably want to name individual cells or cell ranges on your worksheet.

Excel uses the rule that a name in a macro refers to the cell it's specifically linked to. However, if you name a cell, and you can't see the name when you're looking at the cell, you might have problems remembering the cell's name. Conventionally, programmers use a name referring to the cell to the right. But if you start your macro instructions in column A, where can the names go? Obviously, then, if names go in column A, instructions can then go in column B. (Note that if you use names, you also have to use the Formula Define Name command to link the name to the cell it refers to.)

But there's one more element to this structure: comments. *Excel* recognizes something beginning with an equals sign as a command, and ignores everything else. This means you can type just about anything else you like in an adjacent column, and *Excel* will ignore it. And that's where comments should go.

Comments are a very important part of a macro. They describe what an instruction is doing, so someone unfamiliar with the macro can figure out how to work with it. It's important to add comments to a macro, especially if an instruction isn't very obvious.

A macro structured as described above might look like Figure 2-19.

Figure 2-19. Macro Organization

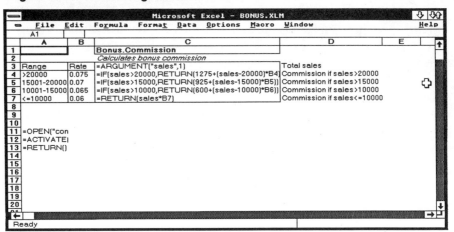

In this example, the standard column width was used for names, but the column width was changed for the instructions column and the comments column was changed to 20 characters, so you'd see everything there.

Note that you can store several macros on one macro sheet or file, and refer to each of them by name. If you have more than one macro on a sheet, use groups of three or four columns for each macro. You can also put macros anywhere on a macro sheet, so the name of the macro (and hence the first line) doesn't always have to be in row 1.

The structure of a macro's logic can be more obvious when you use names to identify program components and comments to explain what's going on. As you mentioned above, names can identify Path A and Path B when there is a conditional branch, and comments can explain how the two paths differ.

It was mentioned earlier that a program can be linear in organization, or contain branches, loops, subroutines, and a number of other elements. It's easier to identify the different parts of a macro's organization if you organize it into tasks, each identifiable with a name and possibly its own entrance point and exit point. The smaller the macro, the easier it is to write. Hence, if you can create a series of small subroutines, each performing only one task or one limited set of tasks, you can shuffle each piece around as you design the macro, until you finally come up with an organization that fits what you're trying to accomplish.

The simplest form of macro is linear: It starts at the top and runs straight down the column until it gets to the RETURN command. The more nearly your subroutines or macro chunks resemble a small linear program, the easier it will be to integrate them into a bigger picture that handles a more complex function.

If you have a situation where your macro needs to evaluate something and make a decision, you have a branching organization that results from an IF command. The syntax of the IF command is presented in detail in Appendix B, and you'll look at branching in more detail in Chapter 5.

If you have a situation that repeats steps until some condition occurs, such as an instruction to *keep printing labels until you've reached the end of the database records,* you'll probably want a loop that uses the FOR, NEXT, WHILE, and possibly the BREAK commands. These commands are also discussed in Appendix B.

If you have a situation where you need to jump from one place to another within your macro, you'll need to learn how to use the GOTO command. That's also discussed in Appendix B.

If you want to run a different macro from within the current macro, you'll use a subroutine organization. To do this, type the macro's name, followed by parentheses, into the appropriate cell on your macro sheet. This "calls" the subroutine. Be sure your subroutine ends with a RETURN statement, so control passes back to the calling macro and continues with the next instruction.

You'll have a chance to look at each of these elements of macro organization in more detail in Chapter 5.

Error Handling

Of course, your macro will execute perfectly the first time, won't it? And it will function flawlessly every time it's used, with no complaints from other users, won't it?

Smart macro programming includes options for things going wrong. What happens if a user enters the wrong data—a part number, rather than its price, for instance? And—let's admit it; it could happen—how should you prepare to deal with a macro that doesn't work the way you intended?

This section will present a few tips for handling errors, things you can use while you're still in the planning stages. Error handling will be discussed in more depth in Chapter 7.

Constructing an INPUT Box

The INPUT command lets you prompt the user for some action. Many input boxes ask the user to enter something: A letter or number, name and address, or something like that. When the Enter key is pressed, that means the input is complete and the characters entered are stored in the active cell.

The syntax of the INPUT command is:

$$= \text{INPUT}(prompt, type, title, default, xposition, yposition)$$

The arguments *prompt* and *type* are required. *Prompt* must be text, and *type* a must be a number. The arguments *title, default, xposition,* and *yposition* are optional; *title* and *default* must be text, and the others are numbers. (Remember that text must be enclosed in double quotes.) The argument *type* identifies the data type:

Value in Argument	Value Type Accepted
0	Formula
1	Number
2	Text
4	Logical
8	Reference
16	Error
64	Array

(You can also enter as *type* the sum of the numbers representing acceptable values. If you enter 5 as the value for type, *Excel* will accept either numbers or logical values.)

The INPUT command produces a dialog box, with whatever was specified as *title* in the bar at the top of the dialog box, and the text specified as *prompt* appearing within the box.

Usually macro programmers use the INPUT command to ask a question. Notice that there's no ability in the INPUT command to make sure input was correct. That responsibility defaults to the macro itself, and suggests that the instruction that follows the macro should check for correct entry.

However, if you write the value in *prompt* with some care, you may be able to prevent some of the errors.

Figure 2-20. INPUT Dialog Box

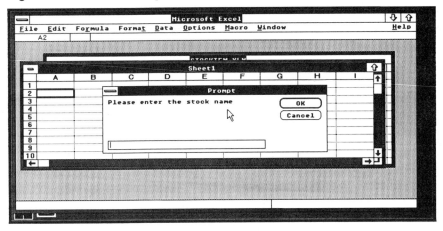

For instance, if you ask a question in the prompt, be sure the question is clearly stated, and that there are a limited number of ways a sensible person could answer it. For example, the prompt

What is your name?

doesn't tell you whether to enter your first name only, first and last name, last name first, or middle initial, or whether to use the appropriate prefix (such as *Mr., Ms., Mrs., Miss,* and so on).

A more appropriate prompt might be:

Enter your first and last name:

Additionally, INPUT commands can contain suggestions as to how you want information handled. For instance, if you want someone to answer a yes/no question with the letter *Y* or the letter *N*, enclose the proper responses in parentheses after the question:

Do you wish to continue? (Y/N)

Be aware, however, that *Excel* will look for whatever value you specify: If you tell it to look for the value *Y*, it will regard as an error the value *YES*, as well as *N* or *NO*.

There's one more thing about using the INPUT command's text: If you expect the user to press the Enter key when data has been entered, say so. In Figure 2-21, below, there's no mistaking what the user is supposed to do.

Figure 2-21. Sample INPUT Dialog Box

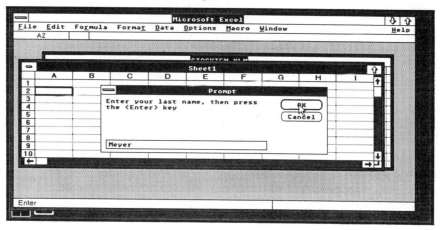

There are two more options to consider with the INPUT dialog box: the OK and Cancel buttons on the right side of the dialog box. If you choose not to enter anything, and choose the OK button, the INPUT command returns the logical value TRUE to the active cell. If you choose Cancel, it returns the logical value FALSE. These returned values offer a chance to opt out of the current data entry. Be sure the instruction following the INPUT command considers all the possible answers coming from this dialog box:

- Correct data entry
- Incorrect data
- OK
- Cancel

(This suggests one or more IF statements, with all the conditions spelled out.)

Using the ALERT Function

One of the ways you can prevent entry errors is to display a message to your user in an ALERT box. The ALERT box displays a

45

message, which may be a question, and expects a response. The syntax of the ALERT command is

= **ALERT**(*messagetext,typenumber*)

The value specified as *typenumber* indicates the type of response expected:

typenumber	Meaning
1	Make a choice (Figure 2-22)
2	Present information (Figure 2-23)
3	Error occurred (Figure 2-24)

An ALERT box lets you tell your user about the consequences of his or her action and, if you use *typenumber* = 1, gives you an opportunity to branch around a trouble spot, perhaps even giving the user a chance to re-enter data. (ALERT returns the logical value TRUE if the OK button is chosen, or FALSE if the Cancel button is chosen.)

A related command, the MESSAGE command, lets you display a message in the status bar at the bottom of the screen. While this doesn't provide the options of the ALERT dialog box, and it isn't as obvious down there at the bottom of the screen, it may be helpful in preventing entry errors.

Figure 2-22. Choice Dialog Box

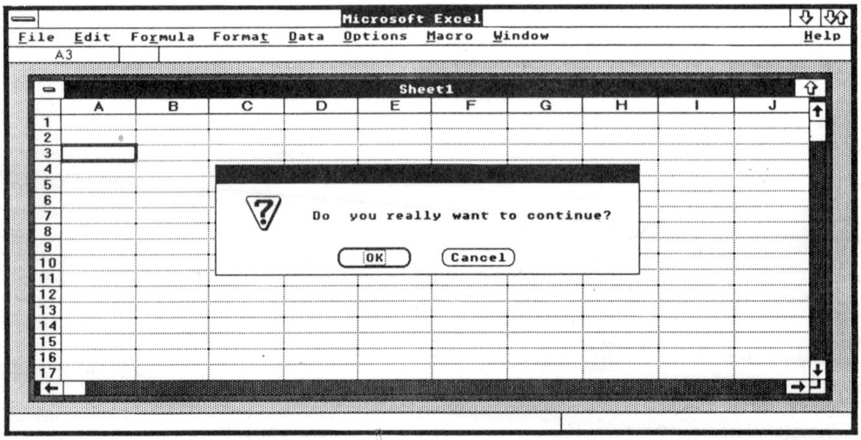

Figure 2-23. Information Dialog Box

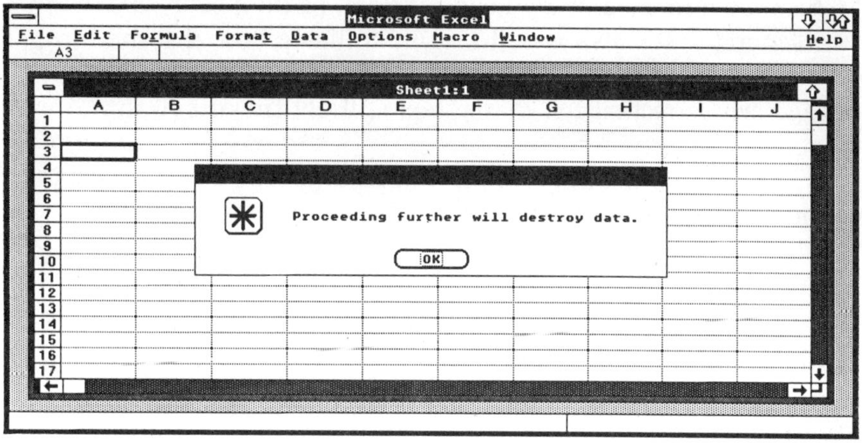

If you use the MESSAGE command, remember to remove it once you're past the steps it's there for, or it will remain on your screen until you quit *Excel*.

Using the BEEP Command

Especially when you're first running your macro, insert a BEEP command to indicate when the macro has completed some section or has passed some event. The BEEP command results in your computer making a sound. The sound will vary, depending on your computer and on the number you specify as the argu-

Figure 2-24. Error Dialog Box

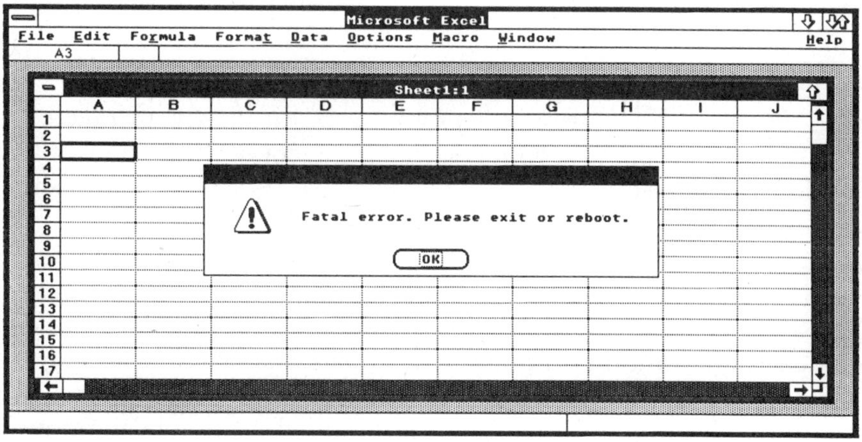

ment for BEEP. As the macro runs, you can keep track of how far it's been able to execute by keeping track of the beeps.

Generally, it's also wise to signal a dialog box or something with a BEEP that requires the user's attention. This way, you're more nearly sure that the dialog box will get the attention needed.

Once you've debugged your macro and are sure it's working as you want, you can delete all but the dialog box beep commands.

You may also want to insert a BEEP command if the user chooses the Cancel option in a dialog box, since doing so generally results in some sort of error condition.

Error Trapping

It will probably help if you devise a subroutine specifically designed to handle error conditions. If you name it, you can then easily branch to it from anywhere in your macro if an error condition is detected.

The ERROR command lets you specify such a branch efficiently. Normally, if an error is encountered when a macro is running, you see a dialog box, letting you choose whether you want to halt the macro, single-step through it, or continue normal running. The ERROR command lets you specify the name or reference of a subroutine that can then be used to deal with errors.

One caveat, however: Use of the ERROR message means *Excel* can't display any of its other messages, including warnings about unsaved documents and the like. Be sure you don't need these messages if you're going to use the ERROR message.

Single-Stepping

Excel gives you a feature that lets you walk through your macro, one step at a time. As mentioned above, encountering an error will let you choose this option. You can also program your macro to proceed this way by inserting the =STEP command in a chunk of macro instructions you want to check. Once *Excel* encounters the STEP command, you'll see a dialog box like the one in Figure 2-25.

The information on the left side shows you which cell is about to be executed, and what that cell contains. The options on the right side let you choose whether to continue single-stepping,

Figure 2-25. STEP Command Dialog Box

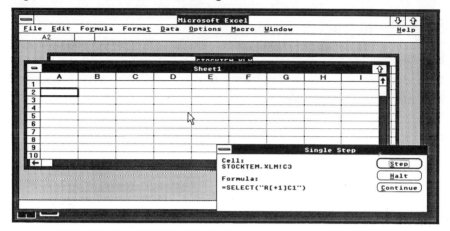

halt execution of the macro entirely, or continue normal execution.

You can also single-step while a macro is executing by pressing the Esc key. A dialog box like the one above appears, letting you decide what to do from there.

Executing a Macro

There are two ways to start execution of a macro. But before either of them can work, the file containing the macro must be open.

To execute a macro on an open macro file:

- Choose the Macro menu, and on it choose the Run command. You'll see a list of macros available on currently open macro sheets. Choose the one you want.
- On an IBM machine, press Ctrl and the shortcut key that corresponds to the macro you want (like Ctrl-A). On a Macintosh, press Option-Command and the shortcut key (like Option-Command-A). The Command key is usually marked on the Macintosh keyboard by a four-leafed clover design. Some newer Macintoshes may also have an "open apple"—the outline of an apple.

The macro will execute its instructions, starting at the active cell on the current worksheet, unless the instructions specify where it is to begin. If the macro doesn't position itself correctly, be sure the active cell is where you want the results of the macro's work to start appearing.

Summary

This chapter has shown you some fairly basic ideas about macros and how to construct them. You've seen how to use the Recorder to create a macro, then how to edit the Recorder's translation of your steps so it becomes more efficient. You've seen some basic kinds of macro structures, and you should have an understanding of the importance of error checking. You've also seen how to execute a macro.

Further chapters will give you more details about constructing and using macros.

Chapter 3
Using the Recorder

Excel has one major component that was included specifically to make it easier for you to create a command macro. Instead of writing your macro as if you were going to write a complex computer program, you can turn on the Macro Recorder function, enter the name for your new macro, and then step through the actions you want your macro to perform. While you're doing this, *Excel* is busy creating a macro sheet that contains the macro equivalent of every one of your commands, line changes, and function calls. When you're finished creating your new macro, turn off the recording function, rename the newly created macro sheet, and save it as a macro file. You may use it again and again.

When you want to use the Recorder to create a macro, first open a worksheet that has the format you want your macro to work with whenever it's used. If your macro is going to work with a blank worksheet, start off with a blank worksheet. If, on the other hand, your macro will be using a worksheet that already contains information or specialized formatting, then have the appropriate kind of worksheet on your screen when you create your macro.

Next, turn on the Recorder. To do this, select the Record command from the Macro menu. Three things happen:

- First, a blank macro sheet is opened. This will happen each time you record a macro, and each macro you record will be recorded onto a separate macro sheet. However, you won't see the macro sheet right away. It's where the macro equivalent of your spreadsheet actions will be stored.
- Next, the recording function is turned on. From this point on, everything you do will be translated into macro statements and recorded on your new blank macro sheet.
- Finally, you are prompted for the name of your macro sheet. This is inserted at the top of column A of your new macro

sheet, as well as having that particular cell designated as a named range on your macro sheet.

Now you're ready to start creating your macro. Simply enter what you want to happen on your worksheet, and each step will be translated into the equivalent macro statements and recorded as part of your macro. You can record text, numbers, formulas, other data, special entries, formatting changes, borders, and anything else you can enter from the keyboard. Moving from cell to cell is also recorded. You might want to note that you aren't recording the literal keystrokes. Instead, you're recording what finally happens to each cell. As a result, if you make a mistake, you can go back and correct it, without having a separate set of alteration commands recorded, so long as you haven't already pressed the Enter key.

Once you're finished recording doing what you want your macro to accomplish, you need to stop the recording process. On the Macro menu, choose the Stop Recording command. You've finished recording your macro.

Once your macro has been recorded, you can do other things with the resulting text. You can edit, format, document, or reconstruct the instruction any way you want. You may note that your cell references are recorded in a strange manner. Most cell references within the text of the macro are absolute references unless you have specified otherwise. But formula references within your macro will be relative cell references, unless you specifically designate them as absolute references.

When you look through your newly created macro, you can see exactly how your keyboard commands have been translated into macro commands. Now you can begin to alter your macro to perform other functions:

- You can create customized menus and dialog boxes that will appear only when your macro is used.
- You can prompt the user for a value using the INPUT function, or prompt the user for other actions using the ALERT and MESSAGE functions.
- You can use the WAIT function to suspend the functioning of your macro for a specific period of time, or use the ON.TIME function to start the macro when a certain time occurs, or when certain data arrives, using the ON.DATA function.

- You can create loops within your macro, so certain actions get performed several times, with the IF-NEXT or WHILE-NEXT functions.
- You can use information about the active worksheet, open windows, cell and file references, names within the current worksheet or any other file to which you have access, to send information to other worksheets or programs using the value-returning macro functions.

The Recorder gives you a simple way to translate your actions into a macro that can then be used over and over, but which can also be modified to perform functions that are far more sophisticated.

Let's see how easy it is to create a macro by recording steps that will automatically generate a simple balance sheet, complete with all the formatting and formulas.

To begin, open a blank worksheet. If you're just starting *Excel*, use the Sheet1 worksheet. If you don't have a blank worksheet on your screen, select the File New command and select the worksheet option.

Turn on the Macro Recorder: Open the Macro menu and select the Record command. *Excel* prompts you to provide a name for your new macro. Instead of the name Record1 (which is the default name *Excel* assumes if you don't give it anything else to work with) use a name that more accurately describes what it

Figure 3-1. A Blank Worksheet

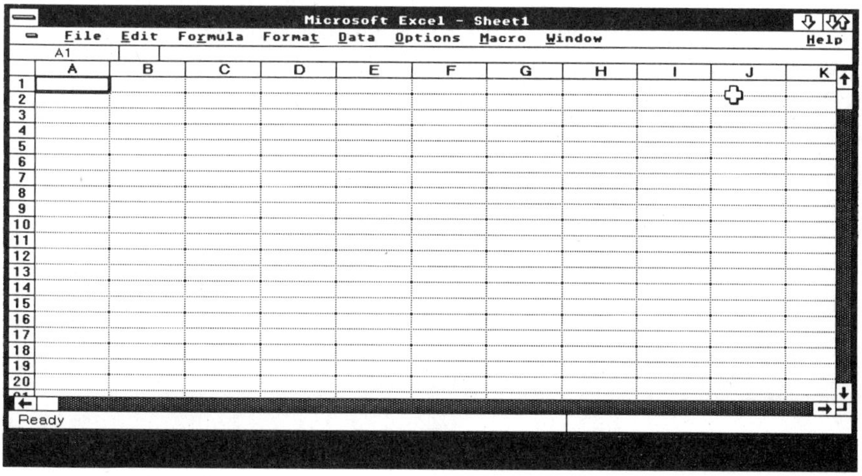

does. In this case, the macro name might be something like *BalanceSheet*.

As soon as you press the Enter key to confirm your macro name, you'll start the Recorder. From this point on, everything you do will be recorded as part of your macro.

Enter the column and row labels for the balance sheet you're going to create. Use the row and column labels you see below. Reformat column A so it has a width of 14. Otherwise, the column is too narrow, and the contents of some cells will spill over into adjacent cells.

Figure 3-2. Row and Column Labels

	A	B	C	D	E	F	G	H
1	Balance Sheet		January	February	March	April	May	June
2								
3	Income							
4								
5	Sales							
6	Rentals							
7	Other							
8								
9	total							
10								
11	Expenditures							
12								
13	Goods							
14	Salaries							
15	rent							
16	Utilities							
17	Office Exp.							
18	Other							
19								
20	total							
21								
22	Taxable Income							
23	Taxes							
24								
25	Net Cash							

Now that you have the labels in place, add formulas. There are a number of formulas that can be simply copied from one cell to another, without your actually having to type them in. However, some of the formulas do indeed need to be typed in. Below is a list of where each formula needs to be entered.

Cell	Formula to Enter
C9	$=SUM(C5:C7)$
C20	$=SUM(C13:C18)$
C22	$=C9-C20$
C23	$=0.2*C22$
C25	$=C22-C23$
D25	$=C25+(D22-D23)$

54

Next, copy the appropriate formulas across into the other cells. Select cell C9 and copy it into cells D9, E9, F9, G9, and H9. As you do this, the copying action will be recorded by the macro. Then copy the following four sets of cells:

Copy C20 into D20 through H20
Copy C22 into D22 through H22
Copy C23 into D23 through H23
Copy D25 into E25 through H25

Figure 3-3. The Completed Balance Sheet

	A	B	C	D	E	F	G	H
1	Balance Sheet		January	February	March	April	May	June
2								
3	Income							
4								
5	Sales							
6	Rentals							
7	Other							
8								
9	total		0	0	0	0	0	0
10								
11	Expenditures							
12								
13	Goods							
14	Salaries							
15	rent							
16	Utilities							
17	Office Exp.							
18	Other							
19								
20	total		0	0	0	0	0	0
21								
22	Taxable Income		0	0	0	0	0	0
23	Taxes		0	0	0	0	0	0
24								
25	Net Cash		0	0	0	0	0	0

When all the cells mentioned above have been copied, you're finished with the actions you need to record in your macro. From now on, whenever you run this macro, it will create a balance sheet for you, ready to be filled in with data.

Now look at your macro sheet, and see all the future typing you've saved yourself. To see the macro, use the Window menu to choose the Macro1 file, which is where your macro was recorded.

Figure 3-4. The Completed Macro

	A
1	BalanceSheet
2	=FORMULA("Balance Sheet")
3	=SELECT("R3C1")
4	=FORMULA("Income")
5	=SELECT("R5C1")
6	=FORMULA("Sales")
7	=SELECT("R6C1")
8	=FORMULA("Rentals")
9	=SELECT("R7C1")
10	=FORMULA("Other")
11	=SELECT("R9C1")
12	=FORMULA("total")
13	=SELECT("R11C1")
14	=FORMULA("Expenditures")
15	=SELECT("R13C1")
16	=FORMULA("Goods")
17	=SELECT("R14C1")
18	=FORMULA("Salaries")
19	=SELECT("R15C1")
20	=FORMULA("rent")
21	=SELECT("R16C1")
22	=FORMULA("Utilities")
23	=SELECT("R17C1")
24	=FORMULA("Office Exp.")
25	=SELECT("R18C1")
26	=FORMULA("Other")
27	=SELECT("R1C3")
28	=FORMULA("January")
29	=SELECT("R1C4")
30	=FORMULA("February")
31	=SELECT("R1C5")
32	=FORMULA("March")
33	=SELECT("R1C6")
34	=FORMULA("April")
35	=SELECT("R1C7")
36	=FORMULA("May")
37	=SELECT("R1C8")
38	=FORMULA("June")
39	=SELECT("R20C1")
40	=FORMULA("total")
41	=SELECT("R22C1")
42	=FORMULA("Taxable Income")
43	=SELECT("R23C1")
44	=FORMULA("Taxes")
45	=SELECT("R25C1")
46	=FORMULA("Net Cash")
47	=COLUMN.WIDTH(14)
48	=SELECT("R9C3")
49	=FORMULA("=SUM(R[-4]C:R[-2]C)")
50	=SELECT("R20C3")
51	=FORMULA("=SUM(R[-7]C:R[-2]C)")
52	=SELECT("R22C3")
53	=FORMULA("=R[-13]C-R[-2]C")
54	=SELECT("R23C3")
55	=FORMULA("=0.2*R[-1]C")
56	=SELECT("R25C3")
57	=FORMULA("=R[-3]C-R[-2]C")
58	=SELECT("R25C4")
59	=FORMULA("=RC[-1]+(R[-3]C-R[-2]C)")
60	=SELECT("R9C3")
61	=COPY()
62	=SELECT("R9C4:R9C8")
63	=PASTE()
64	=CANCEL.COPY()
65	=SELECT("R20C3")
66	=COPY()
67	=SELECT("R20C4:R20C8")
68	=PASTE()
69	=CANCEL.COPY()
70	=SELECT("R22C3")
71	=COPY()
72	=SELECT("R22C4:R22C8")
73	=PASTE()
74	=CANCEL.COPY()
75	=SELECT("R23C3")
76	=COPY()
77	=SELECT("R23C4:R23C8")
78	=PASTE()
79	=CANCEL.COPY()
80	=SELECT("R25C4")
81	=COPY()
82	=SELECT("R25C5:R25C8")
83	=PASTE()
84	=CANCEL.COPY()
85	=RETURN()

Absolute and Relative References

Remember all of those cell ranges you entered in your balance sheet macro? When you entered them, the cell references were in a format like this:

$$= A3 - B3 + C3$$

But look at the macro sheet. The equivalent formula looks quite different. Instead of the A1 format, it looks more like this:

$$= FORMULA(" = R[-3]C - R[-2]C + R[-1]C")$$

The format that appears in a macro sheet is a special reference format that *Excel* uses when it isn't going to know the exact location of a given cell. So, even though it's still a relative cell reference, it winds up appearing quite different from what you might be used to.

Figure 3-5. Macro Cell References

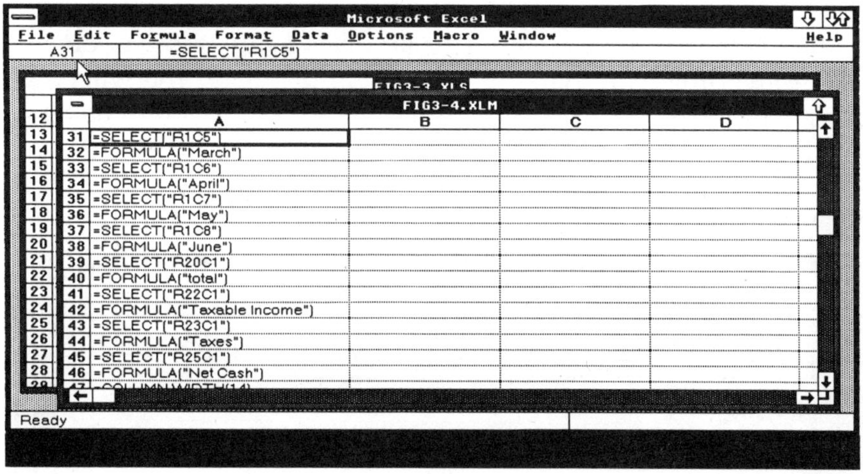

You might also have noticed that the absolute cell references in the macro are formatted differently from fixed cell references in worksheets. Instead of the format you've become accustomed to, such as

$B$4

you can see the fixed references for a cell appearing like this:

R4C2

The reason for this is that, at least insofar as a macro is concerned, a row and a column are virtually identical. The only difference between the two is that rows are labeled with numbers, while columns are labeled with letters. Because of this, *Excel* uses what amounts to an x,y coordinate system within macros, instead of the letter-number locations you might be used to.

When you record a macro, it's normally stored with absolute cell references wherever appropriate, and relative cell references only in those places where you tell *Excel* you want them. As a result, you generally wind up with absolute cell references in functions that call for a specific cell, and relative cell references within your formulas.

If you want to, however, you can use absolute cell references in your formulas. Enter the appropriate cell references (mainly formulas) in the appropriate format on the worksheet as you record it.

You can also use relative cell references throughout your macro, if that's what you prefer. This involves a little more effort than converting to absolute references. In this case, you will quickly discover that you need to tell the Recorder you're using relative references, so it can correctly record your entries.

Figure 3-6. The Macro Menu

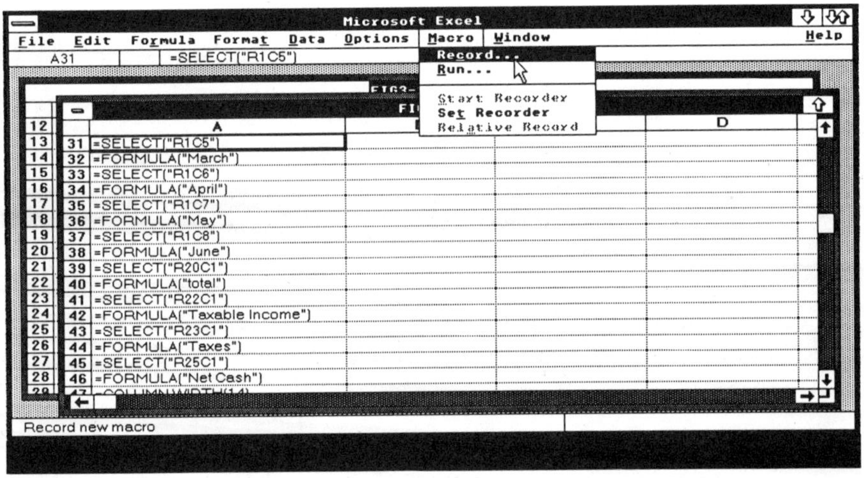

If you've decided you want to use relative references, it actually isn't all that hard to switch from absolute to relative mode, and back again. Whenever you wish to change the recording mode while you're recording your macro, simply open the Macro menu and select either Relative Record or Absolute Record, depending on what is appropriate to where you are. As a result of this, you can toggle back and forth between the two modes while you're in the middle of recording, in case you want a particular part of the macro recorded in a particular format.

Now that you understand the important points of creating a macro, let's change the references so they are relative references, rather than absolute references. This way, the macro can be used anywhere in a worksheet. If the worksheet is kept with absolute references, it will always occupy the same portion of the worksheet, even if there's something else there already.

There are a total of 38 references that need to be altered. Here's a list of the cells in the macro listing that need to be changed, along with the new cell contents.

Cell	New Listing
A3	= SELECT("R[2]C")
A5	= SELECT("R[2]C")
A7	= SELECT("R[1]C")
A9	= SELECT("R[1]C")
A11	= SELECT("R[2]C")
A13	= SELECT("R[2]C")
A15	= SELECT("R[2]C")
A17	= SELECT("R[1]C")
A19	= SELECT("R[1]C")
A21	= SELECT("R[1]C")
A23	= SELECT("R[1]C")
A25	= SELECT("R[1]C")
A27	= SELECT("R[− 17]C[2]")
A29	= SELECT("RC[1]")
A31	= SELECT("RC[1]")
A33	= SELECT("RC[1]")
A35	= SELECT("RC[1]")

(Continued)

59

Cell	New Listing
A37	= SELECT("RC[1]")
A39	= SELECT("R[− 19]C[− 7]")
A41	= SELECT("R[2]C")
A43	= SELECT("R[1]C")
A45	= SELECT("R[2]C")
A48	= SELECT("R[− 16]C[2]")
A50	= SELECT("R[11]C")
A52	= SELECT("R[2]C")
A54	= SELECT("R[1]C")
A56	= SELECT("R[2]C")
A58	= SELECT("RC[1]")
A60	= SELECT("R[− 16]C[− 1]")
A62	= SELECT("RC[1]:RC[5]")
A65	= SELECT("R[11]C")
A67	= SELECT("RC[1]:RC[5]")
A70	= SELECT("R[2]C")
A72	= SELECT("RC[1]:RC[5]")
A75	= SELECT("R[1]C")
A77	= SELECT("RC[1]:RC[5]")
A80	= SELECT("R[2]C")
A82	= SELECT("RC[1]:RC[5]")

In the majority of the cases there's both a row and a column change, indicating that the cursor is moving to a different location. In cells A65, A70, A75, and A80, however, there's only a row change. The reason for this is that when the CANCEL.COPY command is executed, the cursor is returned to the cell from which the copy originated. As a result, you only need to move the cursor down the column containing the original cell entries as opposed to moving it both down and into a new column.

The Recorder Range

Whenever you record a macro onto a macro sheet, you are recording your macro into a region called the *Recorder Range*. This region holds all of your macro in a single column.

Normally, whenever you finish recording a macro, *Excel* defines a new Recorder Range, ready for the next macro. Then, when you start recording the new macro, *Excel* uses that range to record your steps. Unless, of course, you stop working with macros, and shut down *Excel*.

Generally, the Recorder Range will be the first empty column in whatever macro sheet has been specified—the default macro sheet, or one you choose. As a result, if you don't already have a macro sheet open when you start recording, you'll probably record your macro in column A of a new macro sheet.

But if you already have a macro sheet open with a macro in it, you might wind up recording in column F or G, or even further to the right.

Figure 3-7. The Recorder Range on a New Macro Sheet

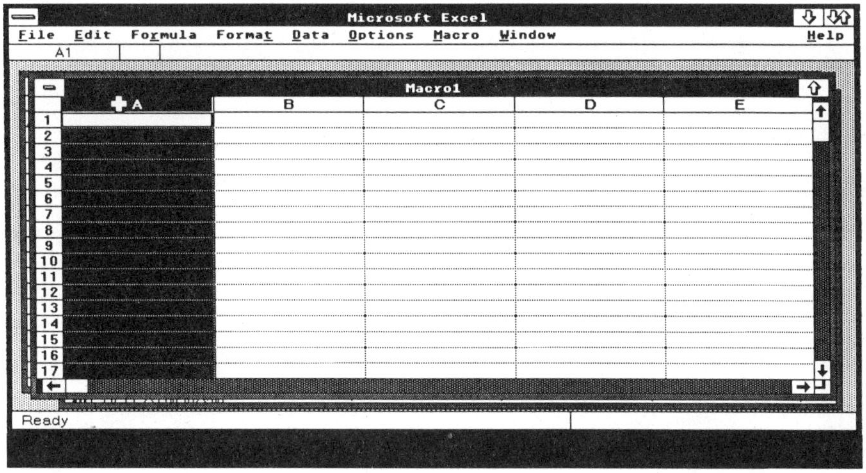

Select column A on a blank macro sheet.

One of the nice things about the Macro Recorder is that you don't have to have a macro sheet open to record a macro. When you start the Macro Recorder, it looks around a little. First, it checks to see if there's a macro Recorder Range already defined. If there is, the Recorder uses that. If there isn't, however, the Recorder checks to see if there's a macro sheet open at all. If there is, it defines the Recorder Range on that sheet, and starts recording your actions. If there isn't any macro sheet open, however, the Recorder opens a new macro sheet and defines the Recorder Range on that sheet before it starts recording. If you want to record a macro onto a new macro sheet, and you already have a macro sheet open when you're ready to make your recording, make certain that the Recorder Range really is defined for the new macro sheet, and not for one you've already used.

You don't necessarily have to use the Recorder Range that's set by *Excel*, however. You may choose one of two ways to set your own Recorder Range on a macro sheet.

The first method requires that there be nothing below where you want the recorded macro to start. If there is anything at all in the rows below it, you are likely to run over the contents of those cells and wipe out some previously created macro.

First, find the macro sheet where you want to record the macro. This can be a new macro sheet, or one already in existence. In either case, once you have the appropriate sheet on your screen, select a single cell on that macro sheet. That cell will be the top row of the macro you record, and your steps will continue to be recorded in the column you've selected until you turn off the Recorder, or the column runs out (which happens somewhere after row 8500—that would be a pretty big macro!).

Figure 3-8. A Starting Cell for a Macro

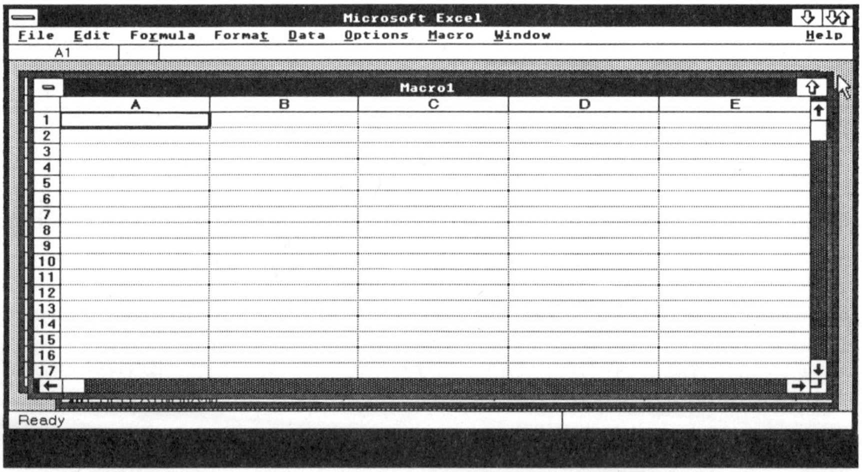

Open the Macro menu and choose the Set Recorder command. This designates that cell as the beginning of the Recorder Range. When you start recording your macro, the macro's name will appear in the cell you selected, and the text of the macro will be stored in the cells below that point.

Where you need to restrict the amount of space available for your macro, there's another way to designate the Recorder Range.

To use this method for recording a macro, first make sure the macro sheet you want to use is displayed on your screen.

Figure 3-9. A Macro Recorder Range

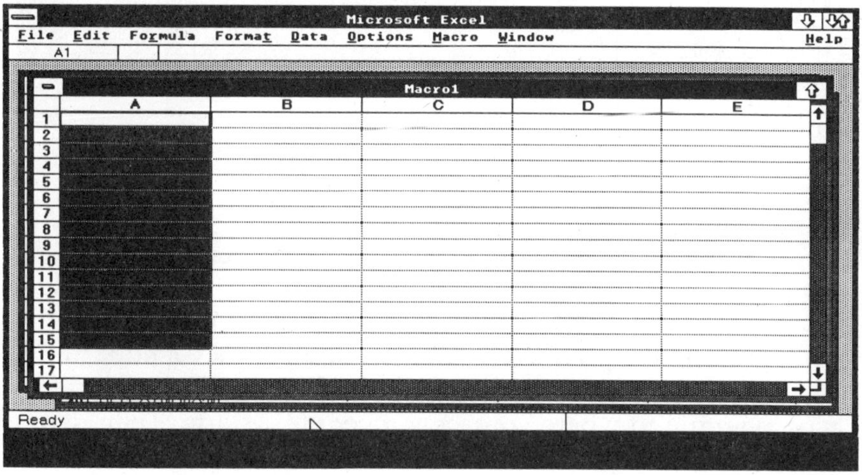

Choose the range of cells on your macro sheet where you want to record the macro. Then, select the Macro Set Recorder command, and the selected range becomes your Recorder Range. Now, when you record a sequence of actions, it will be recorded into that range.

There are, of course, some problems associated with using a limited Recorder Range. The most obvious problem is running out of room while you're recording. When this happens, several things will occur: First, the Macro Recorder function automatically stops. Next, a message appears, telling you that you've filled your Recorder Range (Figure 3-10).

If you want, you can elect to use the macro as it exists, by adding a =RETURN( ) function on the bottom line.

If you aren't satisfied with your macro, however, you can change a few things that will allow you to continue recording.

If there's room below your Recorder Range, you can extend your range so you have more space. To do this, simply redefine the Recorder Range as everything that was previously in the range, plus the new space you want to add.

63

Figure 3-10. Recorder Range Full Message

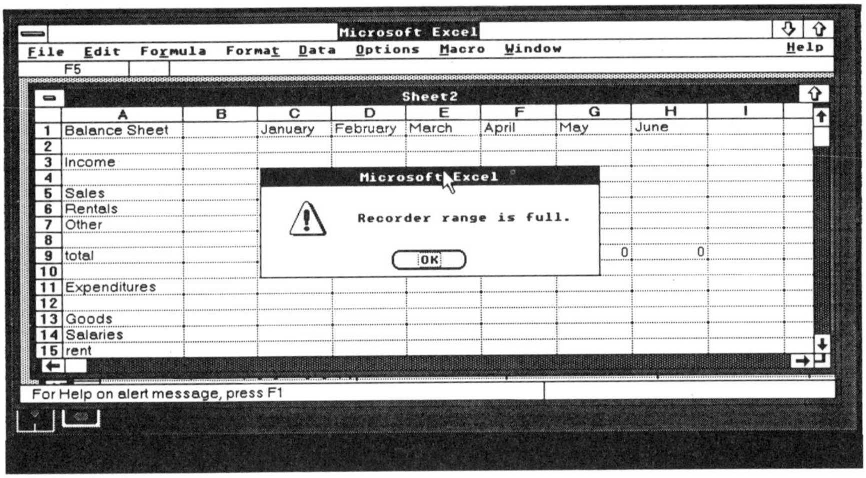

If you can't or don't want to extend the Recorder Range down, you can always move elsewhere and start a backup. In that case, enter a GOTO command at the bottom of your current macro, pointing to where your new macro text starts. Then define the new area as the Recorder Range, and start recording again.

Obedient servant that it is, the Macro Recorder will also record over anything in its path. That might include the text of a macro that already exists in your range. Fortunately, there's a restriction on this ability that will probably save some, if not all, of any macro in harm's way. This restriction is that the first cell in which the Macro Recorder records can only contain one of two types of contents: either nothing, or a =RETURN( ) function. If the initial cell contains anything else, the Recorder will continue looking, further down the range, until it finds a cell that contains a =RETURN( ) or is blank, or until there's no more room. It is important to remember, however, that only the *first cell* of the macro falls under this protection. Once the macro finds a blank cell or a =RETURN( ) cell, anything in a later cell is fair game to be recorded over.

Now you'll see how to use the Recorder Range function to add a macro to your macro sheet that will automatically allow you to generate a summary of each of the different income and expense categories for the six months covered by the macro.

First you need to reset the recording area, so you'll record your new macro on the same macro sheet as the original macro.

To do this, open the macro sheet your original macro was on, and move the cursor to cell B1. Next, open the Macro menu, and select the Set Recorder command.

Figure 3-11. Resetting the Recorder Range

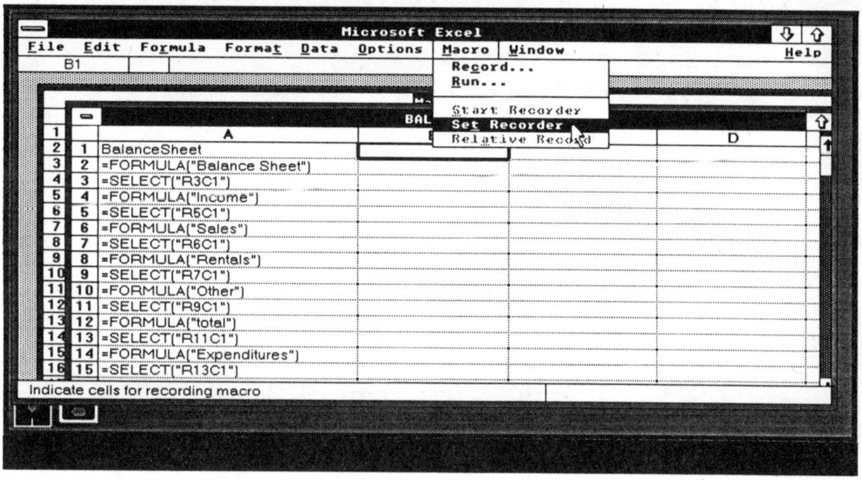

This series of actions will result in all of column B in the current macro sheet being designated as the new Recorder Range. Therefore, when you record your new macro, it will stay on the same macro sheet.

Now you need to create your new macro. If your worksheet (with all the entries you used to make up the first macro) is still around, open it. Otherwise, make sure there's a blank worksheet open on your computer, and run the Balance Sheet macro to re-create the original template. There are two things you'll need to set up prior to recording your macro:

First, move the cursor to the cell two columns over from the June entry on your Balance Sheet worksheet.

Second, open the Macro menu and select the Relative Record command. Now you're ready to create your new macro.

First things first: Start the Macro Recorder, just as you did the last time you recorded a macro. You will again be prompted for a name for your macro, so you should enter a name appropriate to what you're doing, perhaps a name like *Summary*.

Now you should enter the contents of your new macro. The contents will consist of a heading for the column, a series of

=SUM( ) statements, and a single = function. Figure 3-12 shows what they look like, and where they are in relation to each other.

Figure 3-12. Placement and Contents of the Summary Macro

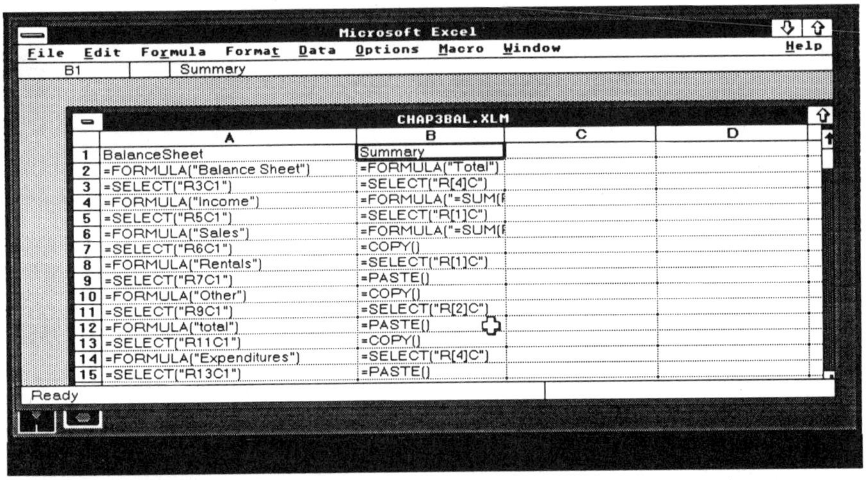

The reason for the = function is that you don't want your summary to have a sum of the net cash. Since net cash is carried forward from month to month, it makes much more sense to just use the final value for the net cash line in your summary.

Now that your macro has been recorded, you'll probably want to clean it up a little. Things like SCROLL functions, while they are necessarily recorded while you're working, are nonetheless rather superfluous to the functioning of the macro. Therefore, you should probably delete all the =VLINE( ) functions from your macro.

What Gets Recorded?

When you're recording a macro, every step of your actions is recorded. But your actions themselves aren't recorded as individual keystrokes. Instead, in most cases, the effect of your actions is recorded. This extends not only to recording the important parts of your actions, but also to dealing with situations where you start something and for some reason don't finish it.

If, for instance, you attempt to execute a command, and it fails for any reason while you are recording, the failed attempt will not be recorded. Similarly, if you start a command and then cancel it for some reason, it won't be recorded. As a result, you can cancel your actions whenever necessary, and not have the equivalent actions show up in your macro.

The actions the Recorder translates for you fall into three basic categories:

- Selecting cells and entering formulas
- Choosing commands
- Opening and closing documents

Selecting cells and entering formulas covers two simple areas:

- Moving about on the spreadsheet
- Entering formulas onto the actual spreadsheet

Movement. Movement around the spreadsheet while working with a macro isn't handled by scrolling around the screen as you normally would. Instead, your macro records only the destination of the cursor, and jumps straight to it.

Formulas. When you're working with a macro, formulas don't just mean mathematical expressions like $=C4+B3/C7$, but also any other action within the spreadsheet. Possibly something like an $=NOW(\ )$ function, or a number or some text you want to enter on your worksheet. If you enter something onto a worksheet, it most probably will appear by way of an $=FUNCTION(\ )$ command.

Commands

When you choose a command from a menu, that specific selection is not recorded. Instead of using the Alt-*menu, command* format you would normally use, each menu command will be translated into a separate and distinct command that *Excel* recognizes as a macro command equivalent.

Opening and closing documents doesn't refer to opening new files through the file menu. Instead, it refers to switching among different files that have already been opened. The action of these selections from the File menu is more like the action of the Window menu.

Since the Recorder operates by recording the essential command in each operation sequentially, any command executed will be recorded, no matter what you do later. Taken to a ludicrous extreme, if you use a command and then use the Edit Undo command to reverse the command's action, the undone action won't disappear from the macro. Instead, it remains, but so does the Undo command, in effect canceling the effect of the command you executed.

While the Macro Recorder can record most actions, it can't be used to create a macro that in turn will use the Macro Recorder during operation.

There are a few other limitations about using the Recorder:

• Whenever you move, size, or scroll a window or dialog box, or change the current selection, all of the appropriate commands are consolidated into just one or two functions so they can operate from the appropriate macro command. As a result, for instance, if you move a window around quite a bit while resizing it, *Excel* records only the final size when the Recorder writes the macro command.
• Whenever you choose the Edit Repeat command, *Excel* simply writes a duplicate copy of the command you are repeating into the macro. The Recorder does not write a separate repeat command into the macro.
• If you are using the File Open command as part of your macro, and you change drives or directories while you're in the process of selecting your file, the Recorder will write a separate Directory function call into the macro, in addition to the File Open command.
• If you are using either the Paste Name or Paste Function commands from the Formula menu, the Recorder will insert a =FUNCTION( ) line into the macro with the appropriate information, instead of recording the appropriate Paste function.

Stopping and Starting the Recorder

Imagine the following scenario: You're deeply involved in recording a macro. Suddenly you discover that you need to get some information from somewhere else. And you don't want that section of what you'll be doing to appear in your macro.

Fortunately, the Macro Recorder lets you do this. First, open the Macro menu, and select the Stop Recorder command (Figure 3-13).

Figure 3-13. The Stop Recorder Command

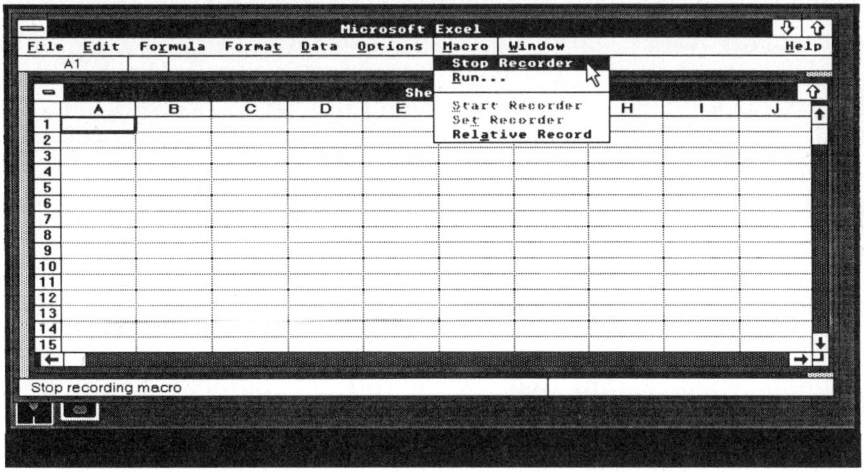

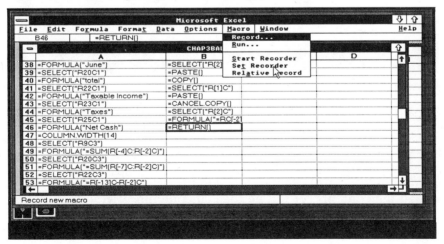

When you execute this command, you're telling *Excel* you want this to be the last point in your macro, so the Recorder stores a =RETURN( ) function as the last line of the current macro.

However, you can fool *Excel* into picking up its recording where it quit, when you finish your diversion.

Figure 3-14. Starting Atop the =RETURN( ) Function

When you stopped recording your macro, *Excel* never reassigned the Recorder Range. It's ready to start again right where it was when you stopped recording your macro.

When you return from your diversion, choose the Macro Start Recorder command if you haven't moved the Recorder Range or closed whatever macro sheet was being used for recording. The Recorder will start again right on top of the =RETURN( ) function that marked the end of your last macro recording session.

Modifying a Recorded Macro

Having finished recording your macro doesn't necessarily mean you're finished creating that macro. You can still do a large number of things with your macro, including adding dialog boxes and prompts, and editing the structure and content of the macro.

Figure 3-15. A Macro-Generated Dialog Box

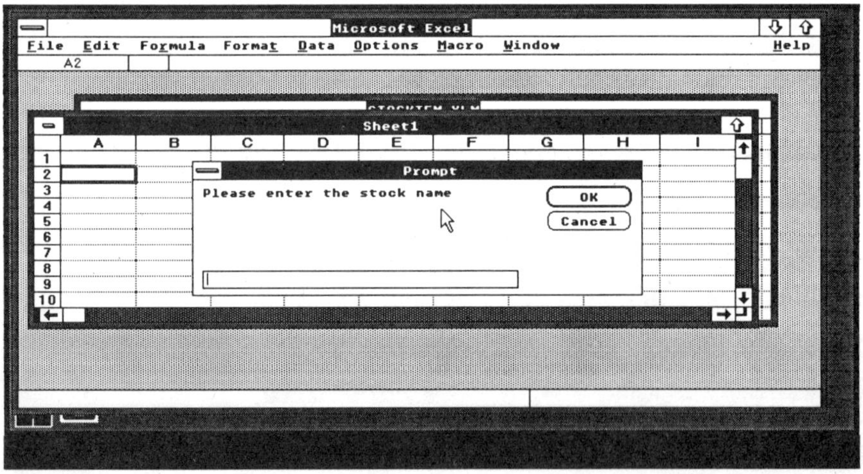

It's important to remember that a recorded macro is the same as a macro that has been generated entirely by hand. Either form can be edited or altered, formatted, moved around, and copied.

Editing a macro works just like any other kind of editing in *Excel*. If you wish to change the contents of a cell, use the F2 key to edit the contents, or retype the cell contents. If you need to add more lines, either use the Move command or the Insert command from the Edit menu.

Figure 3-16. A Macro-Generated Prompt

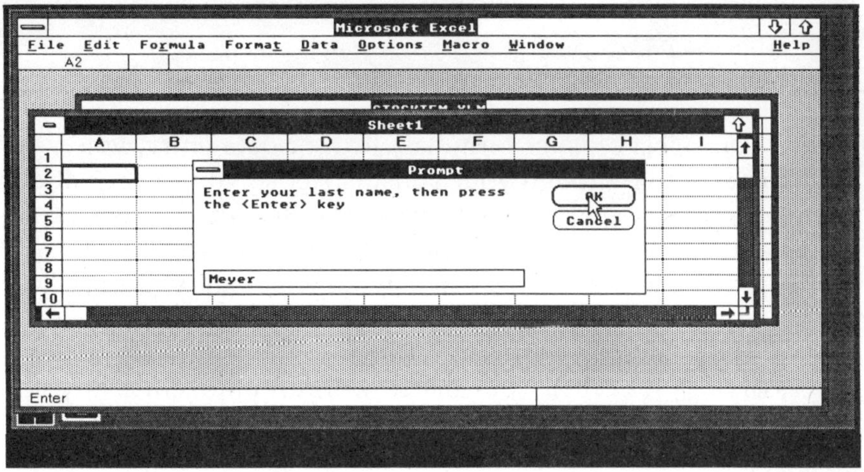

Editing also allows you to add the custom touches to your macro: dialog boxes, prompts, and other forms of "back talk" from the computer can't be recorded—they have to be added after the recording is finished.

The point of recording a macro, however, is to save you the effort of programming the majority of the commands. The Recorder does that for you. This works well: Record as much as possible of the macro by stepping through the actions on a

Figure 3-17. Editing the Contents of a Macro

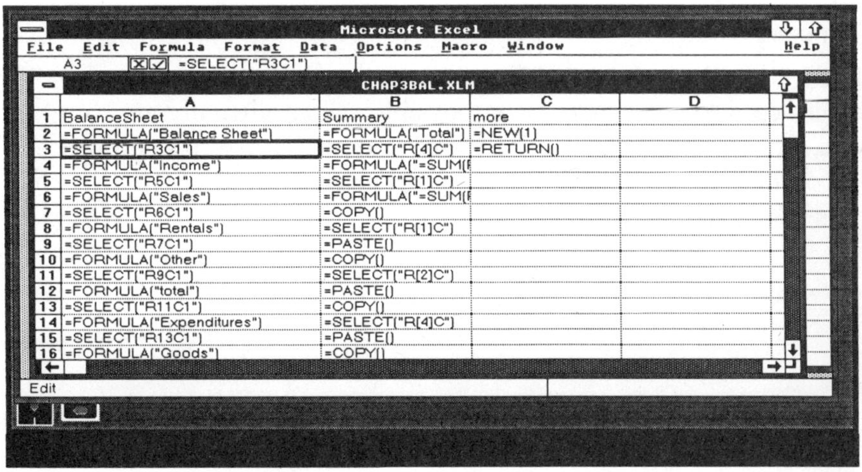

spreadsheet with the Recorder turned on, and then create only those portions of the macro that can't be recorded.

Editing a macro is fairly simple. Here are a few tips:

- When you select cells for formulas, text, or data entry, you sometimes scroll through your spreadsheet so you can see and therefore select the appropriate cells. The Recorder translates this as an application of the =SCROLL( ) macro command. While getting to the desired cell is what you want your macro to do, scrolling isn't necessarily needed if you can get there directly. The =SELECT( ) macro command jumps directly to the necessary cell (or cells). Your macro will run more efficiently if you remove the =SCROLL( ) instructions and only use =SELECT( ) commands.
- Getting a dialog box to work properly can be difficult, at first. If you're going to insert a dialog box in your macro, create a separate macro containing the dialog box, and go through a separate debugging phase with it before incorporating it into the rest of your macro. This reduces potential errors, and also streamlines your work.
- There are actually many situations where creating separate modules will make your work much easier. If each macro segment is programmed separately, it's much easier to find and fix the errors. With fewer instructions in each module, you can more easily correct each module before incorporating the modules into the larger, more complete macro.

Summary

The Macro Recorder has been designed to help you make your macro construction as easy as possible. Since virtually anything you can do with *Excel* can be translated into a macro using the Recorder, you now have a quick and easy method of creating macros at the touch of your keyboard.

Chapter 4
Working with Data and Variables

Excel recognizes six different types of data:

- *Numbers* include both integers and decimal values, and can be positive or negative. Numbers are accurate to 15 digits. You can specify the precision of your numbers (that is, you can specify how many positions to the right of the decimal point your calculations should continue). Numbers include formats like 500, .008, 3.14159, $59.95, 23%, and 9.04e − 12.
- *Text* is one or more characters (a character can be a letter, number, or special character), usually enclosed in double quotation marks. A string of text characters is also known as a character string. Text includes characters like "a," "BANANAS," "Justice O'Connor," "1600 Pennsylvania Avenue," and "206-555-1212."
- *Logical values* are either TRUE or FALSE, but can be stated as 1 or 0, respectively.
- *Arrays* are linked sequences of numbers (for instance, {1,2,3;4, 5,6}).
- *Error values* are error messages stored in individual cells when an error condition occurs (for instance, #DIV/0 when evaluation of formula results in an attempt to divide a number by 0).
- *References* are cell addresses, and can be stated as single cells, cell ranges, or multiple selections in A1 format (C5, $C5,C$5, or $C$5; A1:C5 or $A$1:$C$5) or in R1C1 format (R5C3, R[− 2]C4, R[2]C[− 6], or R6C7:R6C12).

Working with Variables

In a programming context, *data* is anything equivalent to an AS-CII character—the numbers 1, 2, 3, the logical value TRUE, the text strings "July" and "Austin," and the like.

A *variable,* on the other hand, is an indirect reference to data, usually one where the value may change from time to time, depending on other circumstances. For instance, the named cell "Weekday" may contain the time/date number for Tuesday, Thursday, or Friday depending on the formula or macro instructions that reference that cell. In this case, the variable is called "Weekday," and you can use the term "Weekday" anywhere you need whatever data it happens to contain at the moment.

Spreadsheets are generally concerned with data; they produce results based on the snapshot of data and evaluation of formulas at some particular time or under some specified condition. Macros, on the other hand, are more concerned with the general situation in which those data snapshots can take place.

For example, an income statement spreadsheet for the current month will reflect the current figures for income and expenses. The formulas will refer to specific cells by cell address. On the other hand, a macro to compute the income statement will take into account the formulas, but will most likely use names as references for data, which means the incoming data can be stored anywhere, so long as there's a link between the name and the cell address to be used this time.

This use of a name to represent data is a hallmark of a variable, a means of making the reference location-independent so it can be used under more general circumstances. A name representing data values generated during the running of the macro program is stored behind the formulas in the cells of the macro sheet. (They're not literally "behind," of course. As the macro program is compiled, it establishes a link between the memory location containing the data, and the memory location containing the formula. If the value has a name, another link is established between an entry in a table of the names and the memory location containing the data. When the program runs, it follows those links to place values where they're needed.)

Defining New Variables

Excel has two macro functions that assign new values to variables set by a macro program:

- SET.VALUE
- SET.NAME

SET.VALUE. The SET.VALUE function assigns a new value to a cell (or values to a range of cells), and SET.NAME assigns a new value to a name.

SET.VALUE is used any time you want to change the value in a cell, and you're willing to specify it here. The syntax of the SET.VALUE macro function is

SET.VALUE(*reference,values*)

where reference may be a cell or range address in either A1 or R1C1 format, or may be a name referring to a cell or range, and *values* are the values to be assigned to the corresponding address or name.

Whatever is used as *reference,* the reference must be to a cell, range, or name on the macro sheet. (Verify that the name will be recognized by using the Define Name command to display a list of existing names.)

When *Excel* evaluates SET.VALUE, it looks up the cell represented by reference and enters whatever has been given as value in that cell. It doesn't interfere with any formula that may already be in that cell. This makes it especially useful for storing counters when you're looping through some set of instructions.

For instance, suppose you've defined cell D5 with the name *Counter,* and you've initialized it with the formula =1. A common practice when looping through some set of instructions is to add 1 to the counter every time you complete the loop. In this case, the instruction would be

=SET.VALUE(Counter,Counter+1)

This says, in essence, *Find the cell called* Counter *and add 1 to whatever is in there.*

75

Elsewhere in the macro, you can test Counter to see if it contains some arbitrary value, and branch accordingly. A common practice is to follow logic like this:

Decision box: Is Counter => 5?
N: Loop back to top of routine
Y: Return

Figure 4-1. Program Logic Using Counter

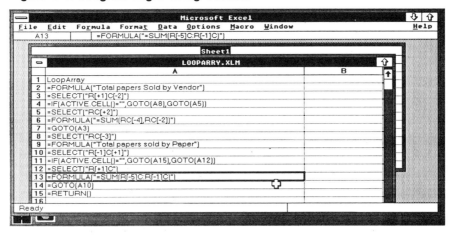

Note, however, that while you've incremented Counter five times before you quit using it, you haven't changed the original formula associated with Counter: When the macro is run again, it will again be initialized to 1.

SET.NAME. The SET.NAME function works in a slightly different way. If you recall how to define names in a worksheet, using the Define Name command on the Formula menu, you remember that a name is always associated with a cell or cell range. The SET.NAME function, however, allows you to use names for values that aren't necessarily associated with a particular location. Like worksheet names, these names are carried along with the macro sheet, but they're used independently of cell location.

The SET.NAME syntax is similar to the SET.VALUE syntax:

=SET.NAME(*"name",value*)

But it works a bit differently. The argument *name* must be expressed as a string (that is, surrounded by double quotation

76

marks). Normally it doesn't refer to a cell location, but in a moment you'll see an example where it can. The argument *value* is the value to be associated with that name.

For instance, you can use the SET.NAME function to establish a value for Counter, just as was done above with SET.VALUE. The initialization is

= SET.NAME("Counter",1)

and the incrementing instruction in the macro is

= SET.NAME("Counter",Counter + 1)

The net effect is the same as that achieved with the SET.VALUE instruction.

However, SET.NAME has another syntax you can use. For instance, these two formulas are the same:

= SET.NAME("Counter",Counter + 1)
Counter = Counter + 1

This means that when you use a counter, or some similar variable, in writing a macro, you can assign values without using either cell locations or macro functions. Be careful with this, however: If you use a named variable without assigning it to a cell, you may not be able to print the results.

Earlier it was mentioned that you can use the SET.NAME function to refer to an address. An example of the way this works is as follows:

= SET.NAME("Total",C5:C19)

With this syntax, the name *Total* is associated with the range C5: C19. This form of the SET.NAME function works much like the Define Name command. However, it too can be expressed in short form:

Total = C5:C19

Here's an example of a macro that uses the SET.VALUE function:

Figure 4-2. Sample Loop Program

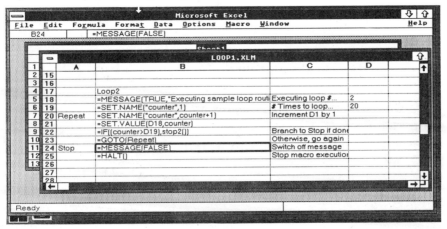

Note that it initializes D2 with a value of 1. It then increments the counter D2 each time it runs through the loop. When it finds that the value of the counter exceeds that of the maximum value (in D3), the IF test tells the macro to stop.

Here's the same macro program, using the SET.NAME function. In this case, we've named the counter that used to be in D2 (now in D19), and in D20 we've referenced it. But if you look at the contents of D20, you won't see a reference to a cell address.

Figure 4-3. Optional Loop Program

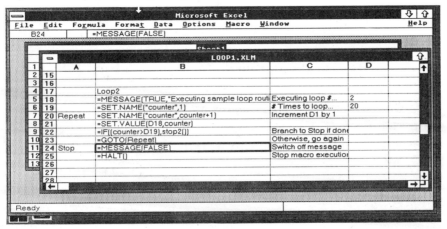

Transferring Data Between a Macro and the Worksheet

Most *Excel* macros assume that when you run a macro, you're doing so on an open worksheet. This means that any calculation done by the macro program will deposit values in worksheet cells. However, you can also transfer data between the worksheet and the macro sheet that opens when the macro program is run. This section will show you how.

The = FORMULA( ) function places a value in the active cell of the current worksheet. You've probably seen it if you've run the Recorder, when you typed either a value or a formula that produced a value.

For instance, these examples all place the value in the parentheses in the currently active cell on the worksheet:

=FORMULA("QUARTERLY SALES")
=FORMULA(3.14159)
=FORMULA(NOW( ))
=FORMULA(Income-Expenses)

However, when used with a macro program, the = FORMULA( ) function can also send the current value of a named variable in the macro program over to the worksheet, storing it in the active cell there.

For instance, if you use the SET.NAME function to name a variable *Augtotal* you can use the following = SELECT( ) and = FORMULA( ) functions to send the value of Augtotal to cell G43, which then is the active cell on the worksheet:

=SELECT("R43C7")
=FORMULA(Augtotal)

You can get a different perspective on the use of the = FORMULA( ) function by looking at a simple macro program. Suppose you need to time individual performance on an exercise by your students. This macro begins running when you press Ctrl-T (on the Macintosh, press Option-Command-T) and records the start time. When you press the Return key, it records the second time and computes the elapsed time. The macro uses the = NOW( ) function and the = FORMAT.NUMBER( ) function to present the time serial number in a readable form. Notice that each recorded time is named, so the elapsed time is determined by subtracting one from the other, and the elapsed time is yet another named time. These names are used by the =FORMULA( ) function to get the three time values from the macro program to the worksheet.

Figure 4-4. Sample Elapsed Time Macro

	A	B	C	D	E
1	timing	time1	time2	time3	time4
2	start=NOW()	=SELECT("R5C2")	=SELECT("R6C2")	=SELECT("R7C2")	=SELECT("R8C2")
3	=ON.KEY("1","timing.xlm!time1")	stu1=NOW()	stu2=NOW()	stu3=NOW()	stu4=NOW()
4	=ON.KEY("2","timing.xlm!time2")	=FORMAT.NUMBER("h:mm:ss")	=FORMAT.NUMBER("h:mm:ss")	=FORMAT.NUMBER("h:mm:ss")	=FORMAT.NUMBER("h:mm:ss")
5	=ON.KEY("3","timing.xlm!time3")	time=stu1-start	time=stu2-start	time=stu3-start	time=stu4-start
6	=ON.KEY("4","timing.xlm!time4")	=FORMULA(time)	=FORMULA(time)	=FORMULA(time)	=FORMULA(time)
7	=ON.KEY("5","timing.xlm!time5")	=ON.KEY("1")	=ON.KEY("2")	=ON.KEY("3")	=ON.KEY("4")
8	=ON.KEY("6","timing.xlm!time6")	=RETURN()	=RETURN()	=RETURN()	=RETURN()
9	=ON.KEY("7","timing.xlm!time7")				
10	=ON.KEY("8","timing.xlm!time8")				
11	=ON.KEY("9","timing.xlm!time9")				
12	=ON.KEY("0","timing.xlm!time10")				
13	=RETURN()				

	F	G	H	I	J	K
1	time5	time6	time7	time8	time9	time10
2	=SELECT("R9C2")	=SELECT("R10C2")	=SELECT("R11C2")	=SELECT("R12C2")	=SELECT("R13C2")	=SELECT("R14C2")
3	stu5=NOW()	stu6=NOW()	stu7=NOW()	stu8=NOW()	stu9=NOW()	stu10=NOW()
4	=FORMAT.NUMBER("h:mm:ss")	=FORMAT.NUMBER("h:mm:ss")	=FORMAT.NUMBER("h:mm:ss")	=FORMAT.NUMBER("h:mm:ss")	=FORMAT.NUMBER("h:mm:ss")	=FORMAT.NUMBER("h:mm:ss")
5	time=stu5-start	time=stu6-start	time=stu7-start	time=stu8-start	time=stu9-start	time=stu10-start
6	=FORMULA(time)	=FORMULA(time)	=FORMULA(time)	=FORMULA(time)	=FORMULA(time)	=FORMULA(time)
7	=ON.KEY("5")	=ON.KEY("6")	=ON.KEY("7")	=ON.KEY("8")	=ON.KEY("9")	=ON.KEY("0")
8	=RETURN()	=RETURN()	=RETURN()	=RETURN()	=RETURN()	=RETURN()
9						
10						
11						
12						
13						

The macro will run wherever you place the active cell on your worksheet, so allow enough room for all the entries. Here's an example where the macro was run on ten students:

Figure 4-5. Timing Macro

80

Each line of the results is the consequence of running the macro once, so you can run it as many times as you need to.

The =ACTIVE.CELL( ) command works in the opposite direction, allowing the macro program to take whatever value is in the active cell of the current worksheet and send it to the macro program.

The =ACTIVE.CELL( ) function actually returns the cell reference, but it's translated to the value stored there. If a formula is stored there, the formula is evaluated and the result is returned to the macro program.

The =SELECT( ) and =ACTIVE.CELL( ) functions are frequently used together, the =SELECT( ) function positioning the active cell, and the ACTIVE.CELL returning the value found there:

=SELECT(R5C8)
Moves active cell to H5
=ACTIVE.CELL( )
Returns value in H5

You can use the =SET.NAME( ) function with the =ACTIVE.CELL( ) function to name the active cell without moving it.

If you want to use the actual reference of the active cell, use the =TEXTREF( ) function:

=TEXTREF(ACTIVE.CELL( ))

This returns the reference of the active cell, as text. =REFTEXT( ) can then convert the text version to a reference.

If you don't want to move the active cell, but you want to use it as a reference point to find another cell and return its value (much like a lookup table or an INDEX function), use the =OFFSET( ) function with =ACTIVE.CELL( ):

=OFFSET(ACTIVE.CELL( ), −5,4)

returns the value in the cell located five columns to the left and four rows down from the active cell.

Using Other Value-Returning Macro Functions

We've already discussed how some macro functions pass values from the worksheet to the macro program, or vice versa. Appendix B lists the macro functions that return values, and describes their arguments and how they work. We'll look at some of them in this section. In all cases, these are functions that return a value from the worksheet to the current step of the macro program, where it can be manipulated and used in further processing.

You've already seen how =ACTIVE.CELL( ), =REFTEXT( ), and =TEXTREF( ) can be used to return and manipulate the contents of the active cell, and how =OFFSET( ) can do the same thing with a cell other than the active cell.

Other cell-related macro functions that return a value are =ABSREF( ), =CALLER( ), =DEREF( ), =GET.CELL( ), =GET.FORMULA( ), =RELREF( ), and =SELECTION( ).

=ABSREF( ) returns the address of the cell that's described in relative terms in its arguments.

=CALLER( ) returns the reference of the cell that started the currently running macro program.

=DEREF( ) returns the value of the cell referenced, but the cell reference must in absolute terms:

=SET.NAME("Fileno",DEREF(!A5))

assigns the value in A5 of the current worksheet to the name "Fileno." (While both =ACTIVE.CELL( ) and =DEREF( ) can return the value in the cell referenced, the difference between them is that =ACTIVE.CELL( ) can alternately return the cell reference itself, depending on how it's used.)

=GET.CELL( ) can also be used to return the contents of the cell referenced in its arguments, but can also be used to return a wide variety of other information about the cell, including row or column identification, formula, format, alignment, border, shading, locked or hidden status, column width and row height, or typeface.

=GET.FORMULA( ) returns the contents of a cell as it would appear in the formula bar.

=RELREF( ) compares two cell addresses and returns the relative reference describing their positioning.

=SELECTION( ) returns the reference of whatever has been selected on the current worksheet, as an external reference. Like =ACTIVE.CELL( ), this reference is usually translated into the value in the selection. For instance, if you've selected B9:B12 on the current worksheet, and that worksheet is named Budget, the

SELECTION function will return Budget!B9:B12 to the macro program.

Two name functions return values: =GET.NAME( ) and =NAMES( ). =GET.NAME( ) returns the definition of what you specify as an argument, as it would appear in the Refers To box of the Define Name command. =NAMES( ) returns a text array of all the names defined on the document you specify as the argument.

The other value-returning functions are more concerned with files, windows, and documents.

=DOCUMENTS( ) returns a text array of all the open documents, in alphabetical order. When used with the =INDEX( ) function, you can use =DOCUMENTS( ) to select individual document names to use in other functions.

=FILES( ) returns a text array of the names of all files in the directory specified in the argument, and like =DOCUMENTS( ), these can be parsed so they can be used individually with functions that take file names.

=GET.BAR( ) returns the number of the active menu bar, which is useful in designing custom menus and dialog boxes.

=GET.CHART.ITEM( ) returns the vertical or horizontal position of a point on a chart.

=GET.DEF( ) returns as text the name of the definition specified in the argument.

=GET.DOCUMENT( ) returns information about the document you specify in the argument. Depending on the code you specify, you can return the name of the document as text, its path name, the type of document, whether it has been changed since last saved, read status, or protection status. If the document is a chart, it will return the type of chart or number of series. If the document is a worksheet or macro sheet, this function will return information about the first and last row used, the number of windows, calculation mode, iteration information, font and size information, numbering system in use, and whether remote referencing is enabled.

=GET.NAME( ) returns the definition of the name specified as it would appear in the Refers To box on the Define Name command.

=GET.NOTE( ) returns the specified number of characters from the note attached to the cell specified in the argument.

=GET.WINDOW( ) returns information about the window

you specify. Depending on the code you specify, you can get the name of the document in the window as text, its number, its x and y position on your screen, its height and width, whether it's hidden, information about what is displayed, and information about the arrangement about panes, if any.

=GET.WORKSPACE( ) returns information about the current workspace, and can return the name or version number of the environment, plus other information describing what is being displayed.

=LINKS( ) returns as text the names of all worksheets linked (by external references) to the document you specify.

=WINDOWS( ) returns as a text array the names of all windows on your screen, and like =FILES( ) and =DOCUMENTS( ) this result can be parsed so you can use individual window names with other functions.

Summary
This chapter has given you a brief look at how *Excel* views and uses data and variables. It has shown you how some of the macro functions handle data passed between a worksheet and a running macro program.

Chapter 5
Program Flow

In earlier chapters it was mentioned that there are a number of ways to structure macro programming. Mostly, however, the structure of your macro will reflect what you're trying to accomplish.

It's important to keep this in mind: How can you make it simple? If this means breaking down your actions into smaller blocks of actions, you'll have several short, easy to follow macros, each with a definite link to the macro that calls it. If this means finding sequences of repeated actions, you'll have a looping structure or a separate subroutine that can be called from several points, depending on what you're trying to accomplish.

Start by writing a verbal description of what your macro is to accomplish. If the actions are simple enough to be described in a single sentence, they can probably be contained in a single macro. If you need several sentences, or you have a complex sentence with several clauses, you probably need several linked macros.

For example, a macro to print something can be simple:

Choose the File Print command, define the area to be printed, and choose the OK button.

Or a print macro can be more complex:

Choose the File Page Setup command, decide whether you want page headers and footers and if so their contents, decide whether you need gridlines and column and row headers, choose the OK button when your Setup menu is complete, choose the File Print command, define the area to be printed, and choose the OK button.

Once you've described what you want your macro to do, deciding about the structure is easier:

Does your macro involve decision-making? Does it involve testing some pointer for a value and taking action based on what it finds? Does it involve determining if a cell has a value or is empty and doing something as a result of what's there?	This kind of situation is a good candidate for an IF function, and a branching structure, which may or may not involve subroutines.
Does your macro repeat certain steps? Does it move to another column and use the same formulas in the same rows?	This is a candidate for a loop structure, in which you use the FOR, NEXT, WHILE, and possibly the BREAK functions.
Does your macro jump forward or backward in the processing, depending on the outcome of certain tests?	This suggests a modular approach, which could involve the naming of certain sections of your macro, or possibly independent subroutines.
Are certain of the calculations specific to one area, where a result could be returned to a cell?	This suggests a separate function macro, rather than the command macros frequently used in a macro program. Function macros can be written separately, like subroutines, and called from within another macro.

This chapter will look at different types of macro structures, and show you when each is appropriate.

Linear Processing

You probably go through some linear processing every day. Perhaps one portion of your day might look like this:

- Drive north on Foothill Expressway.
- Turn right at Page Mill Road.
- Turn right at Hansen Way.
- Turn right into company parking lot.

This kind of flow of action is linear because it goes from step to step, in a straight-ahead manner. There are no decision points, no branching, no detours. It's probably the simplest form of macro program to write.

A linear structured macro looks generally like this:

- Do this
- Do this
- Do this
- Do this
- Stop

When you set up a template for an income statement, such as the one below, the steps you go through are linear. Here's an example of a macro that's designed to just set up an income statement, and wait for you to enter data.

Figure 5-1. Sample Income Statement Template

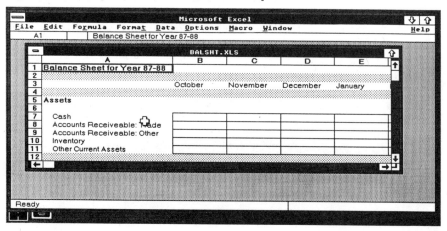

Note that the macro steps do nothing more than repeatedly place the active cell and then put data in the cell, whether the data is text or formulas. There are no decisions, no branching, no detours.

Linear structure is probably the most common form of macro programming. You can create small linear macros to do an enormous variety of special tasks, and use them as you need them, combining the tasks in whatever order is needed at the time.

For instance, here's an example of several small linear macro programs that can be called, one at a time, from another macro. Each performs a specific, limited set of tasks, and because of this they can be combined in any order for a variety of applications.

Figure 5-2. Time/Date Macro

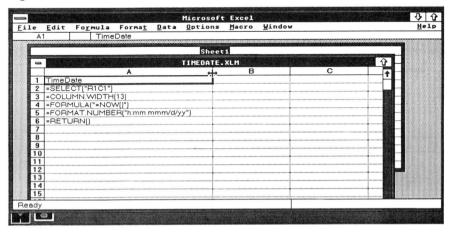

This little macro puts the current time and date in the upper left corner of the worksheet.

Figure 5-3. Boldfont Macro

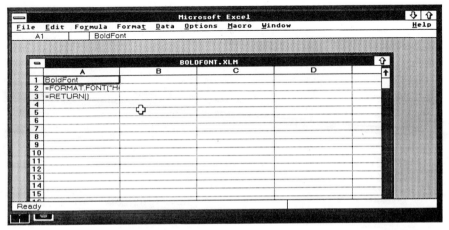

The macro in Figure 5-3, used with text, makes the contents of the current cell boldface.

Figure 5-4. Currency Format Macro

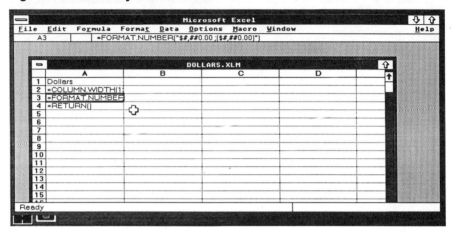

This macro, used with a number, formats the contents of the current cell as currency.

Figure 5-5. Mortgage Payment Macro

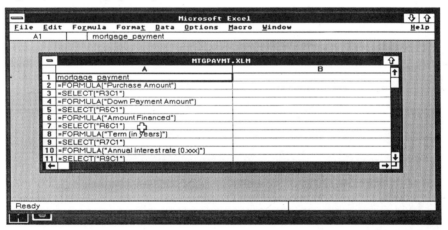

This macro lets you put in the purchase price and down payment for a piece of property, along with the interest rate and term of the potential mortgage, and determines the monthly payment.

Figure 5-6. Mortgage Payment Worksheet

	A	B	C	D	E	F	G	H	I	J
1	Purchase Amount			$225,000						
2										
3	Down Payment Amount			$50,000						
4										
5	Amount Financed			$175,000						
6	Term (in years)			30						
7	Annual interest rate (0.xxx)			11.25%						
8										
9	Monthly payment will be:			$1,699.71						
10										
11										
12										
13										
14										
15										

(Cell reference: D7, value 0.1125)

Notice that each macro performs a small, distinct set of processing tasks, and that each step in each macro follows directly from the actions of the previous step. Typical of linear macro program structure, there are no decision points and no branching.

The Recorder is one very efficient way to create linear structured macro programs, since it steps from cell to cell and performs very specific actions in each. Notice, for instance, in the example below, the Recorder was used to construct a linear structure that sets up a worksheet:

Figure 5-7. Sample Program from the Recorder

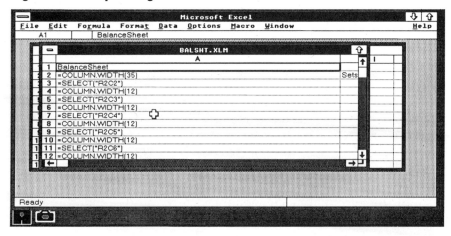

	A
1	BalanceSheet
2	=COLUMN.WIDTH(35)
3	=SELECT("R2C2")
4	=COLUMN.WIDTH(12)
5	=SELECT("R2C3")
6	=COLUMN.WIDTH(12)
7	=SELECT("R2C4")
8	=COLUMN.WIDTH(12)
9	=SELECT("R2C5")
10	=COLUMN.WIDTH(12)
11	=SELECT("R2C6")
12	=COLUMN.WIDTH(12)

(Cell reference: A1, value BalanceSheet; title bar: BALSHT.XLM)

Linear structures are best suited for situations where you're stepping through a straightforward sequence of actions. If you need to make decisions, or test for the presence or absence of something, a linear structure may not be appropriate.

However, as you will see shortly, each of the options you use after a decision point may themselves be linear structures, perhaps separate subroutines, or named sets of macro code that are arranged so they're treated independently.

Conditional Situations

Once you get used to the idea of having a macro program performing some of your spreadsheet work, you will recognize that it can perform some of the decision-making tasks you may have tried to program into a worksheet.

One of the simplest decisions might be something like this:

- Does A5 contain a value greater than 0?
- If so, go ahead.
- If not, stop.

How would you program something like that into a macro? The IF macro statement, like the IF function used on a worksheet, lets you test for the truth value of something and proceed on either of two paths, based on whether the result is true or false. The GOTO statement lets you specify that program logic is to continue at a specific cell.

The syntax of the IF macro statement is:

IF(*logicaltest,truevalue,falsevalue***)**

The value specified as *logicaltest* must be something that can be tested for logical truth. The value can be a cell reference or a name in a formula. Or the logical text can be more esoteric, such as whether the contents of some cell is a number or text, or whether the user has pressed the OK or Cancel buttons on an ALERT box. In any case, with the IF statement, the value so specified must be able to be evaluated as logically as TRUE or FALSE.

Whatever is specified as *truevalue,* and optionally *falsevalue,* must be actions that can be taken. These can include the assignment of values to a cell, range, or name; other macro statements to execute such as a GOTO statement, a warning like a BEEP, or presentation of an ALERT box or MESSAGE line; cell addresses to jump to; or formulas to evaluate.

The syntax of the GOTO statement is:

GOTO(*cellreference*)

The argument *cellreference* can be the address of an actual cell, the name associated with a cell address, or the name of a cell address on another macro sheet.

Notice that there's nothing conditional about a GOTO statement. It absolutely moves control of macro execution to whatever is specified as *cellreference*. However, it's frequently paired with an IF statement this way:

IF(*condition*,GOTO(*point1*),GOTO(*point2*))

where *point1* and *point2* are cell references or names of cell references. You'll see more about the GOTO statement later in this chapter.

Figure 5-8 shows an example of a small macro that uses the IF statement and assigns either of two values to the current cell, depending on what it finds.

Figure 5-8. Sample Macro Using IF Statement

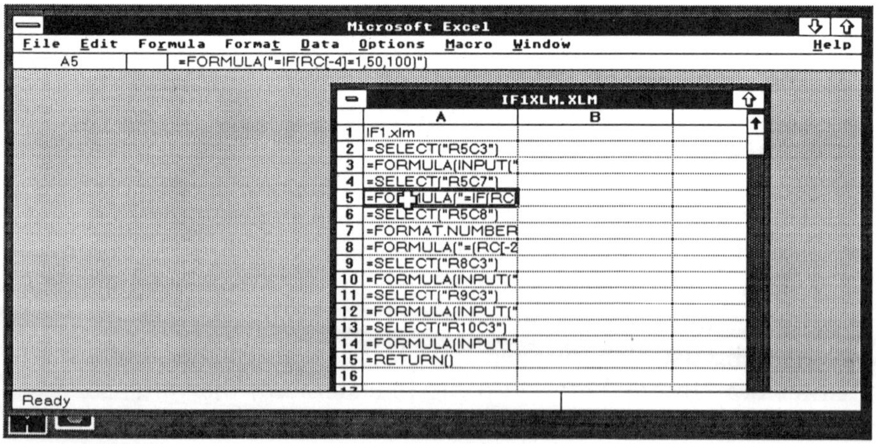

Figure 5-9 shows another example of a macro that uses the IF statement in a slightly different way, this time to test for the value of D3.

Figure 5-9. Sample Macro Using IF Statement

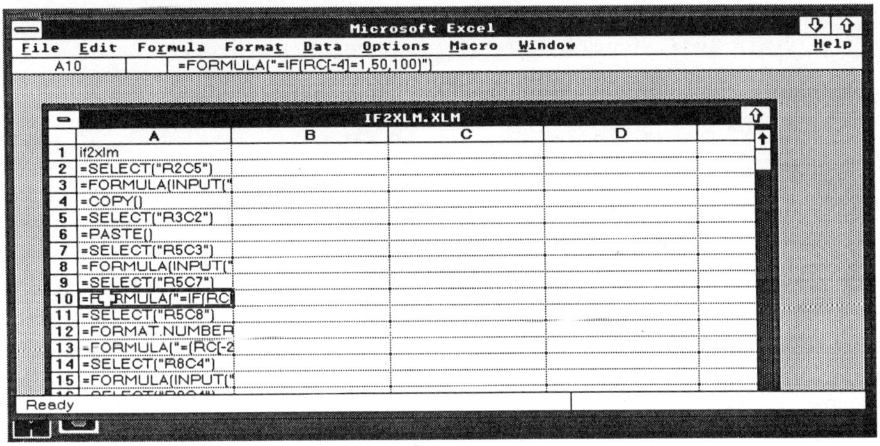

This macro, incidentally, illustrates the use of several macro statements.

The SET.VALUE statement is first used to initialize D2 (in the =SET.VALUE(D2,1) statement), and then is used to increment D2 by one every time the instruction is executed.

Secondly, there is a loop, starting at the SET.VALUE(D2,D2+1) statement named Repeat, and ending with the GOTO(Repeat) statement.

Third, the IF statement in the middle of that loop is the conditional test: It compares the current value of D2 against the desired ending value in D3, and either stops if D2 equals D3, or repeats the loop if the two values aren't yet equal.

An IF statement most commonly tests a counter to see if a maximum value has been reached.

Here's another version of the same type of logic, this time using a named value (in this case, "counter"). Again, the core of the program performs the same loop after initialization of the counter, testing (with the IF statement) whether the counter has reached a value greater than the stop value (in D19).

And here's a third example of the use of the IF statement. Notice that in this example, macro execution continues with the next instruction if the test value is true, and jumps via a GOTO statement to the instruction named Stop if the test value is false.

Figure 5-10. Sample Macro with IF and Jump

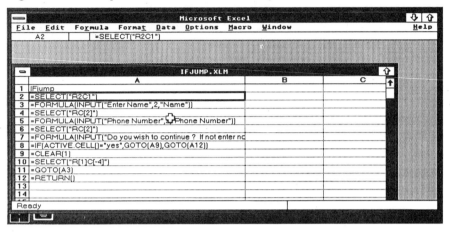

You can also use the IF statement to move to other parts of your macro. Figure 5-11 is an example of the logical structure of this use of the IF statement.

Figure 5-11. Diagram, IF Branch

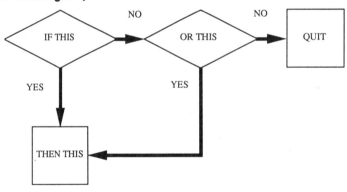

This and the example above are, logically enough, called *branching*. This form of macro structure will be examined in more detail shortly.

The IF statement can be used in a nested approach so you can select from several alternatives. The approach might be like this:

If *x* AND *y* AND *z* THEN *a;* otherwise *b*

The equivalent IF statement is

IF((*x* AND *y* AND *z*),*a,b*).

Or it might look something like this:

If *x* AND *y* THEN *a;* otherwise IF *x* THEN *b;* otherwise *x* THEN *c*

The equivalent IF statement is

IF((*x* AND *y*),*a*,(IF *x,b,c*))

Or it might look something like this:

IF *x* > *y* THEN *a;* otherwise IF *x* < *y* THEN *b;* otherwise *c*

The equivalent IF statement is

IF((*x*>*y*),*a*,(IF((*x*<*y*),*b,c*))

For example, Figure 5-12 is a small macro that positions the active cell in a column depending on the value it finds in the variable named *Pointer*.

Figure 5-12. Cell Positioning Macro Using Nested IF Statements

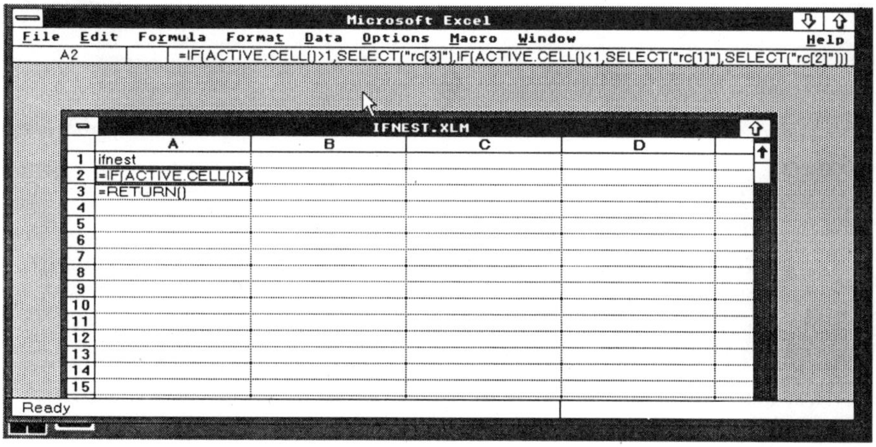

Notice that the IF statements are nested, so the logic is evaluated this way:

- If Pointer is greater than 1, move over three columns.
- If not. . .
- If Pointer is less than 1, move over one column.
- If not, move over two columns.

Note that with the last alternative, you can assume that Pointer = 1. The logic is accomplished totally with the IF and GOTO statements, which illustrates one use of the power of nesting one IF statement within another.

You can also use the IF statement with some of the logical operators, choosing among AND, NOT, and OR. For instance, here's an example of an IF statement that requires two conditions to be TRUE in order to continue processing. If either is FALSE, the macro stops.

Figure 5-13. Sample Macro Using IF and AND

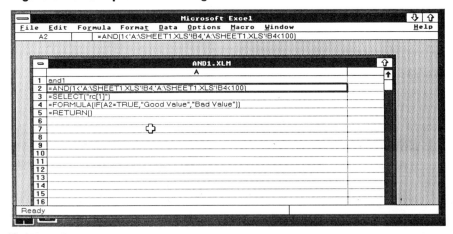

Figure 5-14 is the same macro as Figure 5-13, only it uses the OR statement in place of the AND statement.

Notice that either of the two test conditions can be TRUE for the macro to continue.

Using the IF statement isn't the only way to test a variable. The WHILE statement also tests a variable, but is usually paired with a NEXT statement in a loop. Loops will be covered later in this chapter.

96

Figure 5-14. Sample Macro Using IF and OR

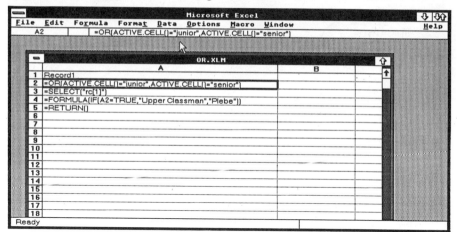

Branching and Subroutines

We looked briefly at a form of branching, using the GOTO statement, earlier in this chapter. *Excel* lets you use a number of forms, including branching to macros that aren't on the current sheet, or branching to a special function macro and coming back right where you left off, or even detouring around some error condition.

When you think of branching, it's important to picture the flow of logic in your macro program as a kind of upside-down tree (Figure 5-15).

Each of the branches represents a program module, and each module is connected to the main program logic. If *Excel* were exactly like this tree, the only way to get from module to module would be through the main program logic, that is, via the "trunk." While macro organization frequently resembles a tree, *Excel* lets you jump from module to module with the GOTO instruction and with several other forms of referencing. We'll look at these in this section.

Branching is a particularly good structure for handling the results of a conditional test. Here's an example of a macro that prompts for input from the user, and then tests to see if what was entered is acceptable (Figure 5-16).

Figure 5-15. Branch Structure

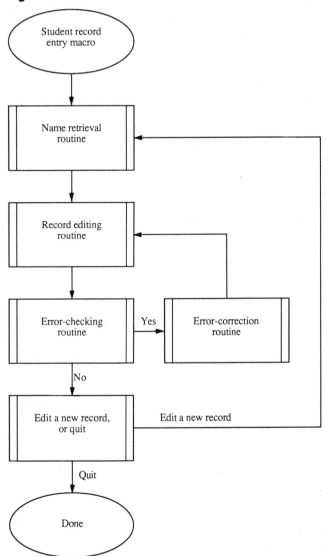

Figure 5-16. Sample Macro Using Input Statement

	Microsoft Excel - XMTGPVMT.XLM			
	File Edit Fo**r**mula Forma**t** **D**ata **O**ptions **M**acro **W**indow			**H**elp
A32	=FORMULA(INPUT("Interest Rate? eg. .065 for 6.5%",1,"Interest"))			

	A	B
14	=FORMAT.NUMBER("$#,##0_;($#,##0)")	
15	=SELECT("R5C4")	
16	=FORMULA("=R[-4]C-R[-2]C")	
17	=SELECT("R6C4")	
18	=FORMAT.NUMBER("0")	
19	=SELECT("R7C4")	
20	=FORMAT.NUMBER("0.00%")	
21	=SELECT("R9C4")	
22	=FORMAT.NUMBER("$#,##0.00_;($#,##0.00)")	
23	=FORMULA("=-PMT(R[-2]C/12,R[-3]C*12,R[-4]C)")	
24	=COLUMN.WIDTH(12)	
25	=SELECT("R1C4")	
26	=FORMULA(INPUT("Enter Purchase Amount",1,"Purchase Price"))	
27	=SELECT("R3C4")	
28	=FORMULA(INPUT("Please enter Down Payment",1,"Down Payment"))	
29	=SELECT("R6C4")	
30	=FORMULA(INPUT("How many years is the Mortgage?",1,"Time"))	
31	=SELECT("R7C4")	
32	=FORMULA(INPUT("Interest Rate? eg. .065 for 6.5%",1,"Interest"))	
33	=RETURN()	

Ready

Notice that if the entry isn't a valid number, the path indicated by the second option in the IF statement resulted in a repeat of the input box. The only way for the macro to continue is for the user to enter a valid number.

This sample was included only to make a point. It's not a good idea to construct a macro that offers only one alternative to entering the wrong data. Humans can make many different kinds of mistakes, and good macro program logic would prompt the user and get the wrong answer a limited number of times before exiting with a warning. Endless loops tend to confuse and frustrate a user.

Figure 5-17 is another example of a macro that prompts the user for input, and tests it for validity. This time, the macro keeps track of the number of times the user enters the wrong information. If after three attempts the right kind of data has still not been entered, the program branches to the instructions that display an Alert box and stop the macro.

Figure 5-17. Sample Macro with Input Statement and Test

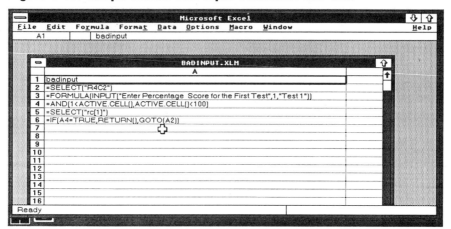

Notice that this program contains only one way to get to the error-processing instructions: You have to fail several times to enter data correctly. However, suppose your macro program were bigger, and contained several other situations where the user was prompted for data, or where processing was tested for the presence of some value. The error-processing section could be used by these separate sets of instructions as well, couldn't it?

The logic involved in this might look something like Figure 5-18.

And this illustrates a point about subroutines: Macro program construction, which lets you call small, utilitarian macros by name, allows you to approach building your macro program from a modular point of view. You and your co-workers can develop a library of small macros, and then use them at will in different applications.

How do you get to them? Simple. Use the GOTO statement. Make sure there's a RETURN statement at the end of each macro you jump to, so control of the program will return to your main logic. Here is the syntax of a GOTO statement that transfers execution to another macro:

GOTO(*Macro1!cellname*)

Figure 5-18. Program Flow, Multiple Entrances to Error-Processing Section

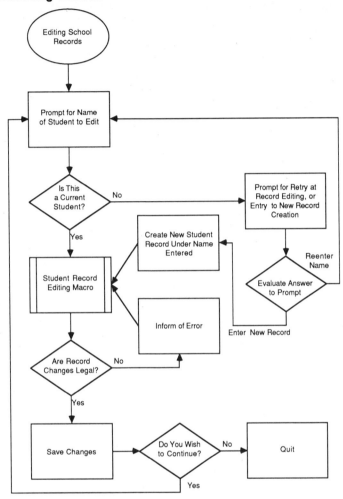

In this case, *Macro1* is the name of another open macro sheet, and *cellname* is the name of a cell in that macro. Notice that the exclamation point is necessary to direct *Excel* to look outside the current macro sheet.

For instance, suppose you have in your library several error-processing macros, each of which takes a different course of action. You can incorporate them all in a new macro program, by calling them from within your new macro logic. (Remember that

Figure 5-19. Macro Logic Using Previously Developed Macros

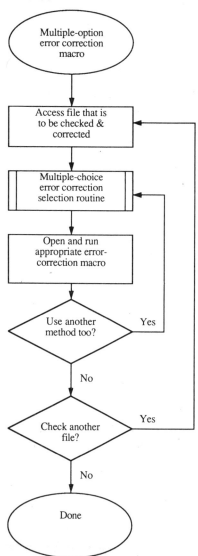

they need to be on open macro sheets when your new macro calls them.) The logic might look something like Figure 5-19.

In this case, the new macro tests for different error conditions (whether the data is numeric, an error value, or something else), and branches to one of three error-processing macros, depending on what it finds. Each of the error-processing macros had been developed earlier, and plugged in here, when needed.

We've tried to show you how small utility macros, perhaps developed by someone else, can be used within your own macro programs, although they don't need to be copied directly into the new macro.

Suppose, however, you have your own small chunks of macro code that can be used from several places within your program. Can you use the same technique?

With reservations, yes. Let's look at an example.

Figure 5-20 shows the instructions for a macro that has embedded within it two small sets of instructions called from several places in the program, depending on several conditions. Notice that the structure of the program looks linear: If everything goes right, execution proceeds directly down the macro. If one kind of error occurs, it jumps over one set of error-processing instructions, and if the other kind of error occurs, only the error processing instructions at the end will be used.

Having the two error routines embedded in the main processing doesn't really contribute to efficient reading of the program logic. The error routines are there to deal with exceptions, not the normal processing. The logical flow would be easier to understand if the user didn't have to consider what happens in the error routines, as well as grasp the logic of the main program.

Providing that the call and return procedures were correct, you could accomplish the same processing if you pulled out the error routines and made them separate macro subroutines. Remember, the call to a separate macro involves the macro name, an exclamation point, and the cell reference. In addition, the subroutine must end with a RETURN statement so execution can return to the calling program.

By making the error routines separate, you'll also make it easier for a user to read them and understand how to use them.

Figure 5-21 shows how the macro sheet might look if you made the two error processing routines separate macro subroutines.

Figure 5-20. Subroutines in Linear Structure

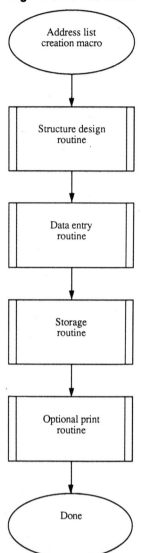

Figure 5-21. Separate Subroutines

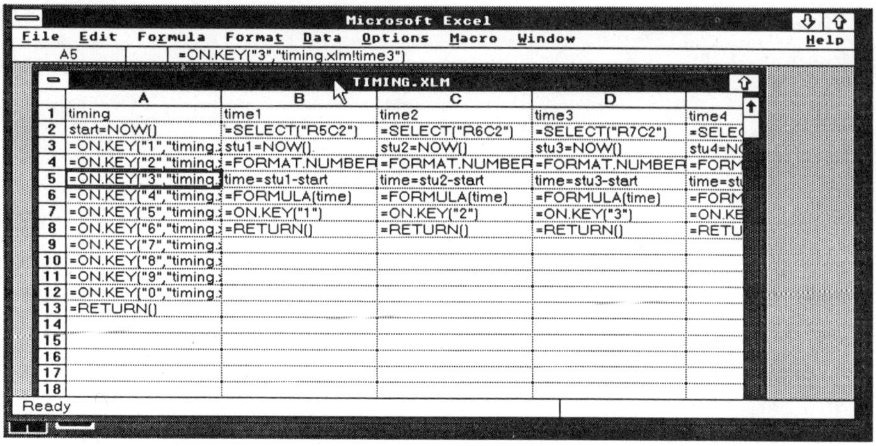

An additional benefit, now that they're stored separately, is that these two macro routines can also be used by other macro programs.

By now you probably have some ideas about how you could approach some of your spreadsheet tasks, using macros that have separate subroutines.

Loops

A loop structure repeats a sequence of instructions until some logical switch changes or some counter reaches a predetermined value.

Two sets of macro statements are used in loop structures. The first involves the WHILE and NEXT statements, and the second involves the FOR and NEXT statements. The WHILE-NEXT structures involve testing a value for the logical values TRUE or FALSE, and the FOR-NEXT structures involve testing a counter for a maximum numerical value.

A WHILE-NEXT loop looks generally like Figure 5-22.

Figure 5-22. WHILE-NEXT Loop

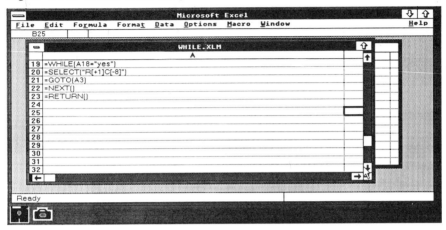

In a WHILE-NEXT loop, you specify a condition that will be TRUE for a period, then become FALSE. While this condition is TRUE, the loop will be repeated. Once the condition becomes FALSE, execution passes to the next statement after the loop.

The sample macro shown in Figure 5-23 demonstrates how a WHILE-NEXT loop works. It averages the test scores of pupils in a class.

The test value, LASTONE, is set to TRUE the first time the macro encounters a student name. The loop computes the average test score for that student, then moves down a row. When it

Figure 5-23. Sample Macro with WHILE-NEXT Loop

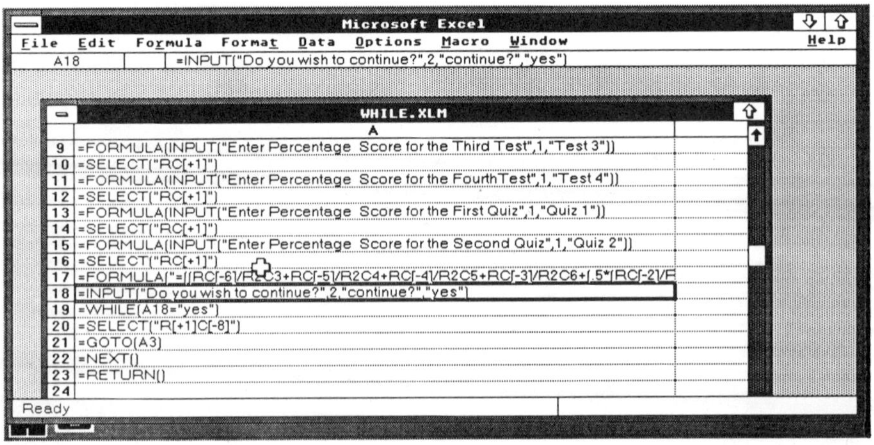

tests the leftmost column for a value, it's looking for a blank cell, which signals that there are no more students. If it encounters a blank cell, it sets LASTONE to FALSE, which allows the macro to exit the loop.

One thing about using WHILE-NEXT loops: The test value must be set to TRUE before the actual loop instructions begin, or macro execution will detour around it, resuming with the instruction after the NEXT statement.

Macros using the FOR-NEXT structure generally look like Figure 5-24.

Figure 5-24. FOR-NEXT Loop

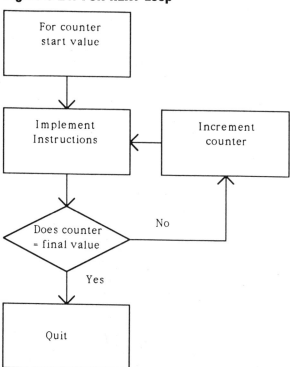

In a FOR-NEXT loop, you need to specify a counter name and its starting value, the increment or step value, and the ending value against which the counter will be tested.

The function of the counter is to keep track of how many times the loop has been run. The step value is added to the counter each time the loop runs, so when the counter has a value equal to or greater than the ending value, the program exits the loop and proceeds with the macro statement following the NEXT instruction.

Figure 5-25 shows an example of a FOR-NEXT loop contained in a macro.

Figure 5-25. Macro with FOR-NEXT Loop

	A	B	C	D	E
1	timing	time1	time2	time3	time4
2	start=NOW()	=SELECT("R5C2")	=SELECT("R6C2")	=SELECT("R7C2")	=SELECT("R8C2")
3	=ON.KEY("1","timing.xlm!time1")	stu1=NOW()	stu2=NOW()	stu3=NOW()	stu4=NOW()
4	=ON.KEY("2","timing.xlm!time2")	=FORMAT.NUMBER("h:mm:ss")	=FORMAT.NUMBER("h:mm:ss")	=FORMAT.NUMBER("h:mm:ss")	=FORMAT.NUMBER("h:mm:ss")
5	=ON.KEY("3","timing.xlm!time3")	time=stu1-start	time=stu2-start	time=stu3-start	time=stu4-start
6	=ON.KEY("4","timing.xlm!time4")	=FORMULA(time)	=FORMULA(time)	=FORMULA(time)	=FORMULA(time)
7	=ON.KEY("5","timing.xlm!time5")	=ON.KEY("1")	=ON.KEY("2")	=ON.KEY("3")	=ON.KEY("4")
8	=ON.KEY("6","timing.xlm!time6")	=RETURN()	=RETURN()	=RETURN()	=RETURN()
9	=ON.KEY("7","timing.xlm!time7")				
10	=ON.KEY("8","timing.xlm!time8")				
11	=ON.KEY("9","timing.xlm!time9")				
12	=ON.KEY("0","timing.xlm!time10")				
13	=RETURN()				

	F	G	H	I	J	K
1	time5	time6	time7	time8	time9	time10
2	=SELECT("R9C2")	=SELECT("R10C2")	=SELECT("R11C2")	=SELECT("R12C2")	=SELECT("R13C2")	=SELECT("R14C2")
3	stu5=NOW()	stu6=NOW()	stu7=NOW()	stu8=NOW()	stu9=NOW()	stu10=NOW()
4	=FORMAT.NUMBER("h:mm:ss")	=FORMAT.NUMBER("h:mm:ss")	=FORMAT.NUMBER("h:mm:ss")	=FORMAT.NUMBER("h:mm:ss")	=FORMAT.NUMBER("h:mm:ss")	=FORMAT.NUMBER("h:mm:ss")
5	time=stu5-start	time=stu6-start	time=stu7-start	time=stu8-start	time=stu9-start	time=stu10-start
6	=FORMULA(time)	=FORMULA(time)	=FORMULA(time)	=FORMULA(time)	=FORMULA(time)	=FORMULA(time)
7	=ON.KEY("5")	=ON.KEY("6")	=ON.KEY("7")	=ON.KEY("8")	=ON.KEY("9")	=ON.KEY("0")
8	=RETURN()	=RETURN()	=RETURN()	=RETURN()	=RETURN()	=RETURN()
9						
10						
11						
12						
13						

Notice that the counter in the macro in Figure 5-25 is defined and initialized within the FOR statement, which means it isn't tied to any specific cell reference. In the sample macro, the loop should move through five iterations, so the ending value is 5.

The NEXT statement defines the end of the loop, just as it did in the WHILE-NEXT loop, so when the loop has been executed, macro execution will resume with the instruction immediately after the NEXT statement.

We used logic much like this when we were discussing using the IF statement and a counter, near the beginning of this chapter. In many ways, loops containing IF statements and a counter resemble FOR-NEXT loops. The difference is that FOR-NEXT loops usually have a very contained structure, starting with the FOR statement and ending at the NEXT statement, and hence are processed quickly, while loops involving IF statements are up to the user to define.

You can nest WHILE-NEXT and FOR-NEXT loops, just as you can nest loops involving IF statements. Each WHILE or FOR statements needs a pairing NEXT statement, demarking the end of that loop. You might wind up with a structure like this:

- WHILE(truevalue)
- FOR(count1,1,3,1)
- FOR(count2,1,5,1)
- macro statement
- macro statement
- macro statement
- NEXT
- NEXT
- NEXT
- RETURN

There is another macro instruction that's useful to have when you're dealing with nested loops. The BREAK statement immediately terminates the loop in which it is located, and is especially useful for error handling. Execution of the macro resumes with the instruction after the NEXT statement that defines that loop.

Function Macros

Most of this book has discussed command macros. Command macros process macro statements that are something like this:

- Position the active cell
- Do this
- Reposition the active cell
- Do this
- Reposition the active cell
- Do this
- Stop

Function macros are a different type of macros in that they perform calculations but can't carry out actions as a result of commands. (You can't use the Recorder to create a function macro.)

Function macros take arguments and return results. They have names, are made up of functions written in cells on a macro sheet, and indeed look a lot like macro functions. However, each function macro does its processing based on the data passed to it in the argument that calls it. How that data gets used is defined in the ARGUMENT statement that begins the function macro.

Function macros use either of two argument forms. The first form,

ARGUMENT(*textname,datanumber***)**

requires that a name be specified for the value of the argument. You may also supply an optional data type number, which we'll define below.

In this form, the name is assigned to the argument corresponding to that ARGUMENT function, for instance:

ARGUMENT. . .
ARGUMENT. . .
ARGUMENT("Price")
ARGUMENT. . .

assigns the name "Price" to the third argument passed to the function macro containing the above list of ARGUMENT statements when the macro is called.

The second form,

ARGUMENT(*textname,datanumber,reference***)**

enters the value of the argument in the cell specified by *reference*. If *textname* is specified, it is assigned to that cell. *Datanumber* is also optional here.

In this form, the value assigned to the argument corresponding to that ARGUMENT function, for example:

ARGUMENT. . .
ARGUMENT. . .
ARGUMENT("Sales", ,D25)
ARGUMENT(. . .

enters the third argument passed to the function macro when the macro is called into cell D25, and names that cell "Sales."

You can pass a number of arguments to the macro when you call it—up to 14 arguments in one call, in fact. There must be an ARGUMENT statement defining what the argument is for each argument. The first argument passed in the call to the macro goes with the first ARGUMENT statement, the second goes with the second ARGUMENT statement, and so forth.

All function macros return a result. You can define what type of data the result will be in either the RESULT statement or in the *datanumber* argument in the ARGUMENT statement. The resulting value is identified by the RETURN statement, which puts the result in the location of the macro function call.

Allowable data type numbers are as follows:

Datanumber	Result
1	Number
2	Text
4	Logical
8	Reference
16	Error
64	Array

You can specify multiple data types by adding the numbers, except for Reference and Array (for instance, the returned value may be a number, text, or logical value if you specify a data number of 7).

The function macro performs the calculations specified in its statements, and returns the value as specified.

For instance, Figure 5-26 is an oversimplified example of a macro that calculates area.

Figure 5-26. Sample Function Macro, Area

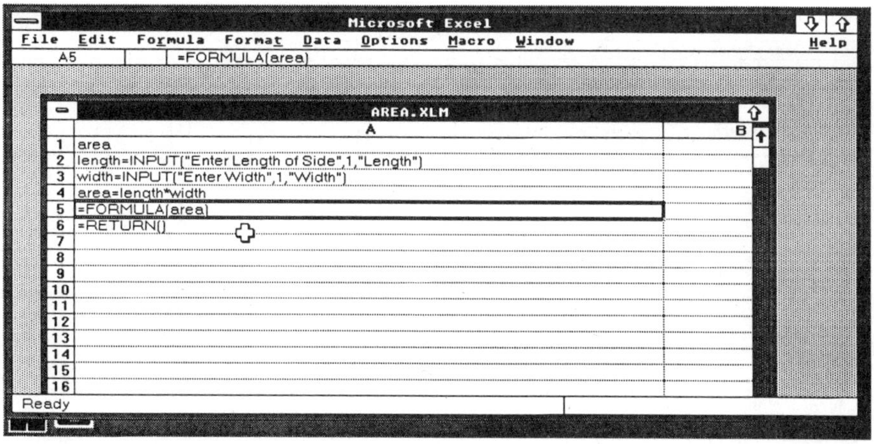

The macro is called with length and width figures necessary for the calculation of the area. The resulting figure, the computed area, is returned in F9.

To call the function macro, specify the macro sheet on which it's located (for example, SURFACE.XLM), and indicate the macro's name and arguments:

=SURFACE.XLM!Area(25,35)

The macro call above will put the figure 875 into cell F9.

Working with Interactive Program Structures

There are several ways your macro can communicate with the user while the macro is running. You can prompt for input with the INPUT command. If the user doesn't enter the kind of data you want, you can display warnings with the ALERT and MESSAGE statements.

Additionally, all the command-equivalent functions that bring up dialog boxes have a form that allows you to use them within a macro. These functions, referred to in Appendix B as Dialog Box Functions, are nothing more than the function name followed by a question mark.

For instance, the Format Alignment command brings up a dialog box (Figure 5-27).

Figure 5-27. Format Alignment Dialog Box

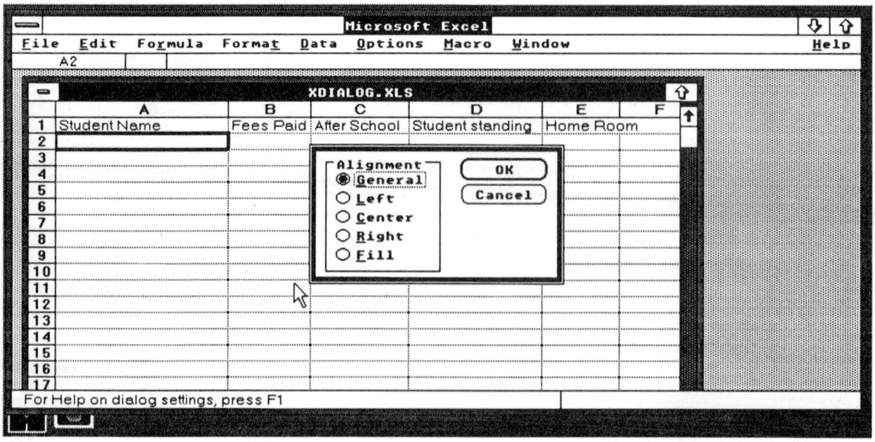

Presented as a macro statement, this command is stated:

ALIGNMENT?

It causes the same dialog box to appear, allowing the user to choose any of the alignment options. The option will apply to whatever worksheet cells are currently selected by the macro.

However, you may wish more extensive interaction, such as having the user type text or a number, a formula, or an array. You prompt for this with the INPUT function. The INPUT command creates a fairly simple dialog box.

Figure 5-28. Sample Dialog Box, INPUT Function

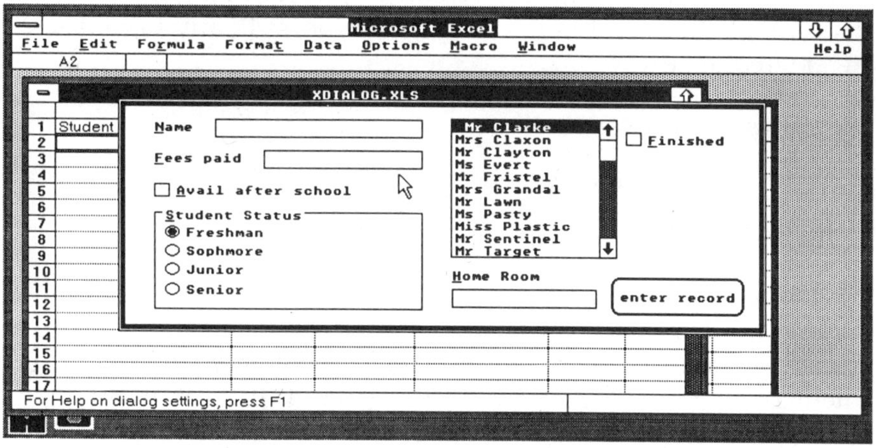

The syntax for the INPUT function is:

INPUT(*prompt,type,title,default,xposition,yposition*)

The arguments *prompt, title,* and *default* must be text; the other arguments must be numbers. Only *prompt* and *type* are required; the other arguments are optional. If you omit *title, Excel* assumes the title is "Input" and this is what appears in the line at the top of the dialog box.

The value specified for *type* is the same set of numbers used as datanumber in the ARGUMENT statement; as used with IN-PUT, they can also be added to indicate the acceptable types of response.

Use of a number in *type* allows you to augment error checking in your macro program. If a value is entered other than the type requested, *Excel* attempts to translate it. If it can't be translated, *Excel* displays its own error message. If you wish to rely on *Excel's* error checking of data input, you may not have to repeat this within your own logic.

What the user types appears in the bar at the bottom of the box. This input can be corrected by backspacing over incorrect characters, or by positioning the cursor where new characters need to be inserted and typing, as long as the OK or Cancel buttons haven't been chosen, or the Enter key hasn't been pressed.

The response to an INPUT statement is entered in the active cell on the worksheet. Percentages get translated to decimal figures (14% becomes 0.14). Cell references, in formulas, for instance, must be stated in R1C1 style. If type = 0, any formulas are entered as text:

"12*(Sales – Commissions)"

instead of the numeric value of

12*(Sales – Commissions).

In the example in Figure 5-29, the INPUT function prompts the user for a student name, and another INPUT function prompts for the test score. A third INPUT statement asks the user whether all student scores have been entered. If "No" is entered, the program loops; if "Yes" is entered, the program exits.

Figure 5-29. Sample Program with INPUT Statement

	A
1	Grader
2	=SELECT("R3C1")
3	=FORMULA(INPUT("Enter Student Name",2,"Student name"))
4	=SELECT("RC[+2]")
5	=FORMULA(INPUT("Enter Percentage Score for the First Test",1,"Test 1"))
6	=SELECT("RC[+1]")
7	=FORMULA(INPUT("Enter Percentage Score for the Second Test",1,"Test 2"))
8	=SELECT("RC[+1]")
9	=FORMULA(INPUT("Enter Percentage Score for the Third Test",1,"Test 3"))
10	=SELECT("RC[+1]")
11	=FORMULA(INPUT("Enter Percentage Score for the FourthTest",1,"Test 4"))
12	=SELECT("RC[+1]")
13	=FORMULA(INPUT("Enter Percentage Score for the First Quiz",1,"Quiz 1"))
14	=SELECT("RC[+1]")
15	=FORMULA(INPUT("Enter Percentage Score for the Second Quiz",1,"Quiz 2"))
16	=SELECT("RC[+1]")
17	=FORMULA("=((RC[-6]/R2C3+RC[-5]/R2C4+RC[-4]/R2C5+RC[-3]/R2C6+(.5*(RC[-2]/R2C7))+(.5*(RC[-1]/R2C8)))/5)*100")
18	=SELECT("RC[+1]")
19	=FORMULA(INPUT("Do you wish to Continue?",2,"Continue","yes"))
20	=IF(ACTIVE.CELL()="yes",GOTO(A21),GOTO(A24))
21	=CLEAR(1)
22	=SELECT("R[+1]C[-9]")
23	=GOTO(A3)
24	=CLEAR(1)
25	=RETURN()

There are a number of customizing functions available within *Excel* that let you create a dialog box or a menu to your own specifications. See the *Functions and Macros* reference manual that accompanies *Excel* for a complete discussion.

The ALERT and MESSAGE statements are also useful for communicating with the user, although the ALERT statement produces a box that allows very limited responses, and the MESSAGE statement allows no direct response.

The syntax of the ALERT statement is:

ALERT(*message,typenumber*)

Anything you enter in place of *message* will appear in the Alert box (the message has to be entered between double quotation marks). *Typenumber* indicates what kind of response is allowed. If *typenumber* is 1, the user may choose OK or Cancel buttons, indicating acceptance or nonacceptance of what *message* describes. If *typenumber* is 2, the only choice is OK, since the purpose of a type 2 Alert box is to present information. A type 3 Alert box indicates that an error has occurred but no choice is available; the accompanying OK button simply means the user has seen the message.

The MESSAGE statement is used to display text in the message area of the status bar at the bottom of the screen. If you use the MESSAGE statement, any system-generated messages will not appear.

The syntax of the MESSAGE statement is

MESSAGE(*toggle,text*)

Whatever is given as *text* is what appears in the status bar. If *toggle* is TRUE, *Excel* displays the message. If it's FALSE, any messages are removed and the status bar is again available to the system. If toggle contains " " (empty text), any messages currently displayed on the status bar are removed.

Use the MESSAGE statement with care. If one of your own messages is there when the system encounters a problem, the system message can't be seen and the user may not know what to do to get the program to work. If you display any message and don't remove it, it will stay there until you quit *Excel*.

You may find one other macro statement useful in interactive applications. The BEEP command sounds a tone. While no response is expected from the user, it is frequently used in situations where you want to get the user's attention, more often than not, to call attention to an ALERT box.

Dealing with Errors

This section deals with *input errors*. Errors in program logic and debugging tools are discussed in Chapter 7.

While most of your work in constructing a macro program is built around the assumption that things will work properly, you should also build in error-checking components to deal with the possibility that things will go wrong.

Earlier in this chapter you saw how some error processing routines could be handled as subroutines. In any lengthy macro it's important that a routine be available to handle situations like these:

- The user enters the wrong data in a dialog box (for instance, a zip code where the phone number is supposed to go, or a social security number instead of an employee number).
- Somehow, the wrong data is passed to a function macro in its calling arguments.
- The macro encounters invalid data in a worksheet cell (for example, the active cell contains text when the macro expects to find numeric data).
- The user chooses Cancel in a dialog box. Is your macro constructed so the information needed can be requested again?
- A command is used where a value is expected, and no values are found. Suppose your macro expects to find a numeric value (0 would be acceptable), but instead encounters a blank cell. Does your macro logic take this possibility into account?

Error-processing subroutines help your macro recover from situations like those described above. While there is no one specific way to write an error processing subroutine, the important thing to remember is that all possible wrong actions need to be covered, either through your own subroutines or by system error messages.

One of the easiest ways to deal with problems with values is to take advantage of the error messages statements ISERR and

ISERROR. ISERR checks whatever is specified as its argument for any error value but #N/A, and ISERROR checks its argument for any error value at all. A common use of either of these statements is frequently structured like this:

IF(ISERROR(C5,GOTO(Errmacro),RETURN)

If there is an error value in C5, the macro branches to the error-processing macro named Errmacro; otherwise it returns to the calling instruction.

There is no one correct way to write an error processing subroutine. It's simply another macro, or portion of a macro, and needs the same kinds of structural considerations as any other set of macro statements. A good error subroutine should, however, either halt macro execution, take an appropriate detour, or warn the user about invalid data.

Summary

This chapter has discussed several types of macro structure, showing you how to use linear, conditional, branching, and looping structures. It has also showed you how to use *Excel* macro commands to create dialog and ALERT boxes, and discussed the importance of providing for errors when your macro is executed.

Chapter 6
Working with Other Files

Excel is designed to share data with a variety of other programs. An *Excel* worksheet can use information from other worksheets, other programs running under *Windows,* other Microsoft products, and even a number of non-Microsoft programs. In addition, *Excel* can use data acquired from other computers, using a Local Area Network, a direct connection, or a modem. This chapter will show you some of the ways you can use *Excel* macros to import and export data.

Using Other Files

Excel can use a wide variety of data formats in the worksheets and charts it generates. In addition to using data from other *Excel* files on your computer, you can use data from other programs designed to run under *Windows,* programs that aren't designed to run under *Windows* at all, and in some cases from completely different computer systems.

When you decide to work with data from another file, it's important to determine just what format the data stored in that other file is encoded in. For example, if you're using PC *Excel,* and you want your macro to retrieve data from a Macintosh *Excel* file, you won't have any problem for the simple reason that both Macintosh and PC *Excel* use the same file storage format. Conversely, if you're going to use data from a *Lotus 1-2-3* file (identified by the .WKS or .WK1 file formats) you would need to make sure your copy of *Excel* was capable of understanding *Lotus 1-2-3* files.

Fortunately, both the Macintosh and PC versions of *Excel* have been designed to make use of networks and other file-transfer methods. As a result, there are format-translation capabilities that wouldn't at first seem to make sense, such as the ability of Macintosh *Excel* to accept *Lotus 1-2-3* files, or the capability of PC *Excel* to accept and use various Macintosh files, as well as both version's capacity to use the .CSV format (Comma Separated

Figure 6-1. Importing a Lotus 1-2-3 Spreadsheet

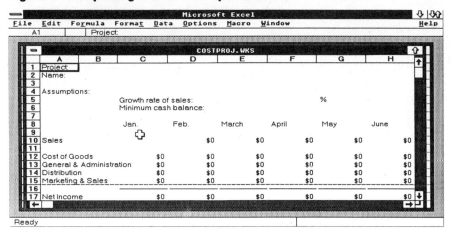

Values), a data storage format used by a number of spreadsheet packages.

Similarly, if you're going to be importing database information into a worksheet, determine in advance that *Excel* can handle information formatted that way. If it can't, you may need to create a decoding/parsing macro to help you import and translate the information.

But databases and other spreadsheet programs aren't the only file types *Excel* can work with. In addition, any file that has been stored as tab-delimited text (.TXT format), or uses the Symbolic Link (.SLK or SYLK format) or the Data Interchange Format (.DIF format) can be understood easily by *Excel*. All these file formats are common enough, some being generated by particular word processors, others by computers using specific software management packages, such as *Windows* or GIF, and still others are used as the standard data format on certain computers, most notably the Macintosh.

Using Linked Files

The File Links command illustrates one of the most useful methods of using other *Excel* files: file links. These special references allow you to retrieve information from other files for use in an *Excel* worksheet, or conversely to retrieve information from *Excel* files for some completely different program.

119

There are two truly effective methods of using linked files. The first of these is the *workspace file.* The second is the *Calculate Now* command.

Unfortunately, the workspace file is a relatively recent development. As a result, *Excel* version 1.5 for the Macintosh doesn't include this useful innovation. Hopefully, when the next version of *Excel* is released, workspace files will have been included.

A workspace file is actually more than just a single file. It's a collection of files, arranged in the order they were in when they were saved. As a result, workspaces are a very useful method of dealing with linked files. Instead of accessing an individual file, you can have your macro work with a whole series of linked files.

A good example of this is the quarterly sales report workspace contained in the PC *Excel* Library subdirectory. This set of files appears on the Macintosh in the Sampler folder. The files in this workspace include the main quarterly sales report and four separate local sales reports.

Figure 6-2. QUARTER.XLW Workspace

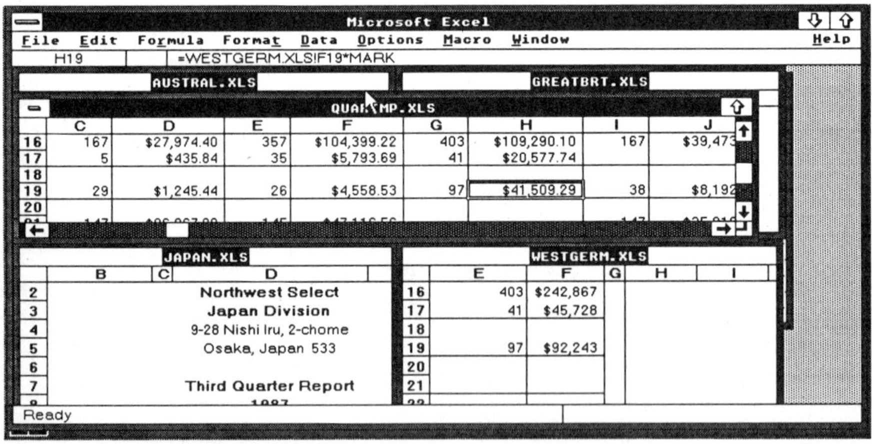

In this set of files, each of the individual sales reports (AUSTRAL.XLS, GREATBRT.XLS, JAPAN.XLS, and WESTGERM.XLS in PC *Excel*, AUSTRALIA, GREAT BRITAIN, JAPAN, and WEST GERMANY in Macintosh *Excel)* are linked into the main quarterly sales report (QUARTMP.XLS in PC *Excel*, QUARTER3 in Macintosh *Excel).* Whenever the QUARTER.XLW workspace is opened, each of these files is also opened, so the complete quarterly sales report can be viewed.

The standard format *Excel* uses to refer to an external file is to have a exclamation mark as part of the filename listing. As a result, an external reference in the IBM environment would look something like this:

= "C:\WINDOWS\LIBRARY\AUSTRAL.XLS"!E14

While the Macintosh version would appear like this:

= ':AUSTRALIA'!E14

In each case, the external reference appears to be so much gibberish. In fact, once you know what each component means, it's quite easy to piece together exactly where the reference is pointing.

=	In both cases, this means that this entry is a function, and should be treated as a function instead of as a text entry.
" " or ' '	This is the boundary for a file name. In the IBM environment, the " " is used, while the Macintosh version uses a ' '. In either case, the appropriate quotation marks should appear just before and after the end of each filename.
C:\WINDOWS \LIBRARY\AUSTRAL.XLS	This is a PC *Excel* reference to a particular file. When it is working with DOS files, *Excel* uses the standard conventions for describing a file, including disk and directory names.

:AUSTRALIA

This is a reference to a Macintosh-format file. Instead of using the "disk:\directory\ subdirectory\filename" convention, the Macintosh version of *Excel* uses a colon (:) to denote a file or folder change, and then lists the file or folder name.

!E14

This is used to tell *Excel* the location of the cell you're interested in, within the appropriate file. The exclamation point (!) is used to distinguish an external reference from an internal one.

In each case, once the individual elements of the syntax have been mastered, it's relatively simple to make sense of the entire formula.

One thing to remember is that you can establish a file link to more than just another *Excel* file. You can also use file links in the IBM environment to get information from other *Windows*-compatible programs, such as *Microsoft Word*. In addition, if you're using MultiFinder on the Macintosh, you can get data from other programs by suspending the operation of *Excel*, and starting another application.

Using Unlinked File Data

Unlinked files can also be used as data resources by your macros, in much the same manner as linked files were. If you use an unlinked file as a data source, your macro will be oriented toward retrieving and using data from another file, rather than creating and using a link.

The first and most notable difference is that your unlinked file data may well require parsing, and most definitely will require more creativity in how you pass the data from one file to another. Instead of merely selecting the cells that contain your data and then linking those cells into the file you want to receive the information, you will need to provide a range where your macro can copy the data, or direct-access functions that retrieve those portions or aspects of the data in which you are interested.

Figure 6-3. A Direct Access Function

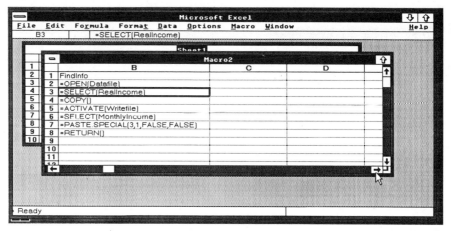

You might notice that this function doesn't use many actual cell references. Instead, named ranges are used. The macro that works with this function extracts portions of a data file into a series of named ranges on the same worksheet that contains the function.

As you can see, the function has a number of named ranges it doesn't use. This is because the macro is designed for a more

Figure 6-4. Listing of Named Variables

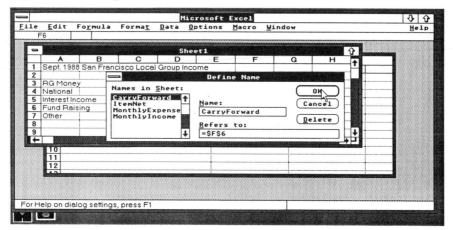

generic application. As a result, there are a number of named
ranges in the file only because the macro needs them, not because the functions in the worksheet need them.

Figure 6-5. Value Lookup Macro

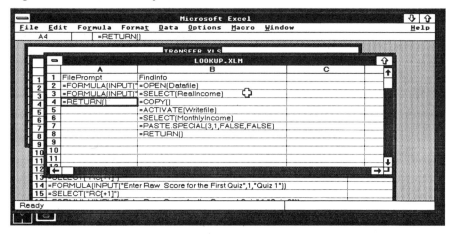

As you might have noticed, the structure of the macro is actually fairly simple. All you need to do is make sure your data file
uses the correct format and the file you want the values stored in
has certain named values defined. If this is the case, simply run

Figure 6-6. Filename Input Box

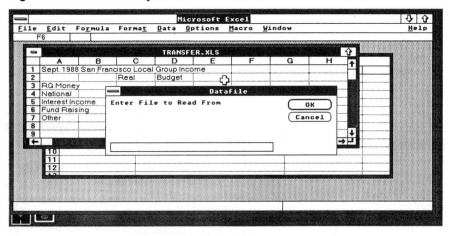

the macro. After you've entered the name of the worksheet from which you want to retrieve data and the worksheet where you want the data put, the macro will do the rest.

This type of macro actually has a few advantages over linked files. When you are using linked files, unless the file you're retrieving the data from is open, it's impossible to see the actual values each reference uses. If you use unlinked files, however, the values are always there. If you wish to use a different data source, the values can be changed by simply rerunning the macro.

A variant of this type of macro mentioned at the beginning of this section uses a range of empty cells in the file receiving the data instead of a named range. Instead of copying the values from the data file into a named value, this type of macro simply copies the value (or whatever value you want from among several values) into one or more of the cells in your *data range*.

Both of these types of macros do have one limitation unless you're willing to engage in some very creative programming. Specifically, they require that both the data file and the worksheet receiving the data be in a particular format, and that they already contain certain items. The only real way to get around this necessity is to program the macro with the intelligence to translate your data file format into a format that makes more sense to you and your computer.

Figure 6-7. Sample Parsing Macro

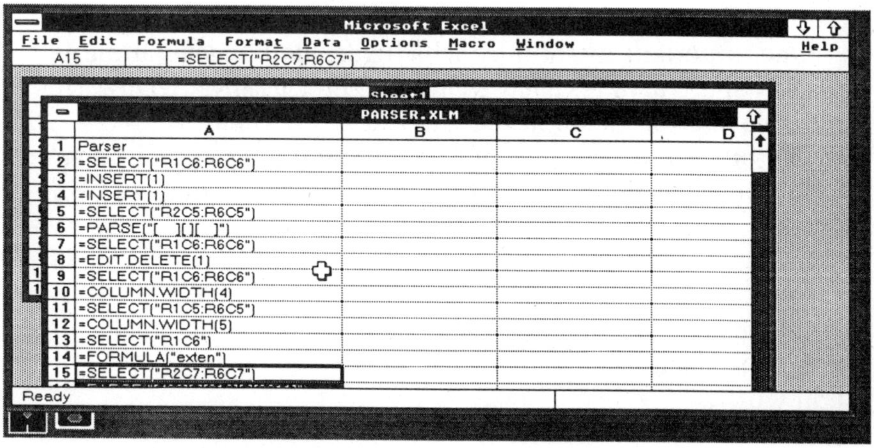

Working with Files from Other Programs

At this time, there really isn't any way for Macintosh *Excel* to use data from a completely different program, except by way of the Clipboard. If you're going to use the Clipboard to transfer data, simply copy or move the data you want shifted into the Clipboard, start *Excel,* and paste the data into your worksheet.

In an IBM environment, however, you can use data from other programs with *Excel* as either one value or a series of cell values. If the other program you wish to use operates under *Windows* for the PC, you can also establish file links from that program to your current worksheet. You can also use data from another IBM program even if it doesn't operate under *Windows.*

It's possible to link a worksheet to a file created by another program running under *Windows.* Both applications must be running under *Microsoft Windows,* version 2.0 or higher, however. The program doesn't necessarily have to be from Microsoft, but it must meet the requirements for *Windows* environments; most programs that do meet these requirements will usually have some mention to this effect in either the User's Guide or some other documentation.

We won't go into any detail here about running other programs under *Windows* 2.0. The basic concepts of windowing, both with files and different applications, are covered in the *Excel* Reference manual under the *Windows* topic. The whole point of running the other programs under *Windows* is so they can share the Clipboard and other similar utilities and so the file access method is one *Excel* can use.

One important method by which various *Windows* applications can share data is called *Dynamic Data Exchange* (DDE). This topic is covered in detail in the *Excel Reference Guide.*

The other main method of exchanging data is the Clipboard, a facility in *Windows* that temporarily stores data while it's being moved or copied from one application to another. There are several Clipboard commands often referred to in this book:

- Edit Copy
- Edit Copy Picture
- Edit Cut
- Edit Paste

To use data from another program running under *Windows,* it must, at some point, become data that can be stored in a cell. If it's numeric data, it has to be in a form *Excel* can eventually work with. This might require that you use one or more of *Excel's* functions or the Data Parse command to manipulate it into a usable form.

For example, if a date is buried in a text string in your incoming data, you may want to use some of the text-processing functions to strip the other data away, leaving just the date, and possibly use one of the date functions to store the date in a format *Excel* can use.

In most cases, however, numeric data is stored in format *Excel* can use. As a result, you can directly link to the supporting data.

When linking to a file created with a non-*Excel* program, but running under *Windows,* the procedure is similar to linking to another *Excel* file:

1. Open both the worksheet and the non-*Excel* file to which you wish to link.
2. Activate the document window of the file you want to link.
3. Select the cell, range, value, or field of the data you want to use, and choose Edit Copy.
4. Activate the worksheet window.
5. Position the active cell where you want the incoming data to go.
6. Choose Edit Paste Link.

Excel establishes the link with a formula that follows specific conventions, using this form:

='APPLICATION_NAME' | 'DOCUMENT_NAME ' !reference

Each portion of the formula tells *Excel* something about how to find the data you want.

APPLICATION_NAME

Must be immediately preceded by an equals sign and immediately followed by a vertical bar (|). The application name must either be a legal *Excel* name or be enclosed in single quotes. In the example above, we enclosed *APPLICATION_ NAME* in quotes to make it acceptable to *Excel*.

A vertical bar must separate the application name and the document name. It's used to tell *Excel* that what follows is not just a different *Excel* directory.

'DOCUMENT_NAME'

Must be the name of the file in the other application. (Some applications, particularly some network servers, consider documents to be "topics"; in that case, use the "topic" name here.) This name can be up to 255 characters long, and may include the full path name, the name of a terminal, and any opening parameters necessary for *Excel* to use to get to the document you want. If there's any question about *Excel* being able to understand the document name (perhaps because of the presence of some characters required at the other end, but which *Excel* considers illegal), enclose the document name in single quotes.

!	Separates the document name from the cell reference or value.
reference	Is the cell, range, name, value, or field of data you want to use. What goes here can be a cell or range address, the name of the cell or range, the value you want to use, or the reference to the datafield (in a database, for instance) containing the information you want to use. We have discussed cell referencing methods elsewhere. If the name of the data looks like a cell reference (for instance, IF38, which could be taken to be the cell on row 38 in column IF, or may be the name of a value derived when some condition reaches 38), enclose it in single quotes.

The procedure for opening and updating a worksheet linked to another application is very similar to that used in opening an updating another linked *Excel* worksheet. When you open a worksheet containing remote references to another application, *Excel* asks you if you want to reestablish links to that other application. Answer *Yes* if you want the current values for those links; answer *No* if you want to use the last values received from that application during this session.

If *Excel* tries to establish a link and fails (the supporting application isn't running, or can't be accessed), *Excel* asks if you want to start the application. If you agree, *Excel* tries to start the application; if it can't, the cells with external references to this application display the #REF! error value.

Converting Data from Another Program into an Excel File

You can open and save files using the formats

.XLS, .XLC, .XLM, .XLW
.TXT
.CSV
.SLK
.WKS, .WK1
.DIF
.DBF

These formats are accepted by *Excel* as valid. In some cases, you may need further conversion (using the Macro Translation Assistant for *Lotus 1-2-3* macros, for instance). Generally, however, if it's a spreadsheet or database file in one of the above formats, you can use the data directly in *Excel.*

You use one of these files simply by opening it. *Excel* may ask you how you want to use it; specify that it's a worksheet file if that's how the data is stored, or a chart file if that's what is in the file.

You can also use *Excel* files in other applications. To do so, simply use the File Save As command and choose the correct filename extension. Note, however, that *Excel* charts don't convert correctly into *Lotus 1-2-3* charts.

Figure 6-8. Unsuccessful Conversion Window

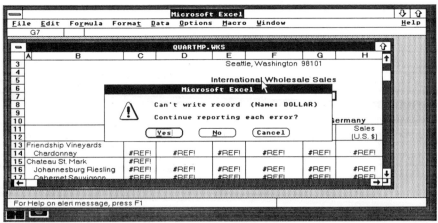

When *Excel* opens a file with one of the non-*Excel* formats, it tries to convert the formulas into formats *Excel* recognizes. If it can't, you'll see a message giving the cell references involved. Write these down on a piece of scratch paper so you can go back and modify them later. This same message asks if you want to see the next formula that can't be converted. If you continue to answer *Yes*, you'll see all the places in the file where *Excel* couldn't successfully convert a formula. When *Excel* finishes the list, or if you answer *No*, *Excel* tells you how many formulas it didn't convert—in other words, the number of cells where there are formulas you'll need to fix. When a formula couldn't be converted, *Excel* preserves the previous value of the formula.

You can also convert files from *Excel* for the Macintosh to files using the MS-DOS version of *Excel*. Worksheet files coming from the Macintosh must have been saved as SLK files. Cell attributes (formulas, values, formatting, protection status), names, calculation settings, and display settings (displaying or hiding gridlines, row and column headings) are converted. Window characteristics, such as window size, position, split, the location of the current cell, and the position of scroll bars, and printing formats such as margins, headers and footers, are not converted.

SLK worksheet files coming from *Multiplan* can also be used by *Excel*. As with Macintosh *Excel*, the cell attributes, functions, and names are converted, while window and some printing characteristics are not. If some of the formulas can't be converted, you'll see messages indicating the location of these cells.

Chapter 7
Debugging and Editing Your Macros

Unfortunately, despite our most thorough plans, some macros don't work the first time they're run. While initially that's a rather demoralizing turn of events, most programmers come to realize that finding and fixing errors within their programs is a necessary and useful part of development.

How do you approach the task of making your macro program work correctly?

Start by realizing that many macro errors are the result of very simple mistakes: a misspelled name, the wrong cell reference, a typographical error in a macro statement, a missing argument, or even a missing parenthesis. Many of the more obvious mistakes of this sort will be caught by *Excel* as they're typed, with onscreen warnings and a beep. The more subtle mistakes, as some infamous textbooks are fond of saying, are left as an exercise for the reader. Lucky you.

For instance, can you spot the errors in this set of macro statements?

```
=SELECT(R5C3)
=FORMULA("NOW( )")
=SELECT(R6C3)
=FORMULA("1/1/90")
=SELECT(R7C3)
=FORMULA("R[−1]C − R[−2]C")
=RETURN
```

It seems so straightforward. In C5 there is today's date. In C6 there is the date Jan. 1, 1990. In C7 you're determining the difference between the two dates. Nice and simple. The exception is that each of the SELECT statements is supposed to enclose the cell references in double quotation marks *and* parentheses, like this:

= SELECT("R5C3")

and each of the FORMULA statements is supposed to have an equals sign between the left parenthesis and the first set of quotation marks, like this:

= FORMULA(= "NOW( )")

Left in its original form, what would have appeared in C5 would have been the text string *NOW( )* rather than a date value.

It's easy to miss errors like these. That's one type of error you can find and fix during the debugging process.

Some macro errors are more complicated. They may involve wrong assumptions about the contents of a given cell at some point in the macro's execution, or wrong assumptions about the results of some operation. Some errors may be even more devious, and may require you to research exactly how *Excel* handles certain kinds of data when passing and processing variables.

But how do you find all these errors? And once you've found them, how do you fix them?

Start by recognizing that debugging is a separate but vital stage in the development of your macro, and that testing it rigorously will help you find errors so your users won't have to. It's much better to discover computation errors in a payroll macro while it's in the debugging stage than when it's run for the first time in a real-time situation and 50 angry employees are complaining about the figures on their payroll checks.

Begin the debugging and testing process by saving at least two copies of the macro as it was developed, designating one as the version to be used in debugging. Use this version as your test version, since in the finding and fixing process you'll be changing the logic.

As you make changes to the logic, document what you've done, and save each changed version. A common approach is to use the last one or two characters of the filename as a kind of revision version counter: *payrolla, payrollb, payrollc,* and so forth. Add comments in the column to the right of the macro instructions or at the bottom, indicating what's different about this version from previous versions.

This approach is extremely helpful when you encounter another problem common to the debugging process: In the process of fixing one problem, you create another. By changing one instruction so it creates the proper immediate result, you also create an error later on in the program. However, when you've saved the earlier versions of your macro, you can go back and see how the program handled the situation before you changed the instruction. This may give you ideas for alternate solutions.

The Debugging Process

Generally the debugging process means fixing the obvious mistakes, then testing the program as rigorously as time allows to unearth the not-so-obvious mistakes, and fixing those.

Fixing a macro statement is as easy as changing something on a worksheet. Macro statements are nothing more than formulas contained in cells, and hence can use the same editing tools used with spreadsheets. This means that, once the cell is selected, you can backspace over the characters, deleting the wrong ones and adding new ones. You can also insert and delete cells the same way you do on a worksheet, or clear the contents.

If you need help remembering the syntax of a particular function, use the Help menu. In an IBM environment, the Help menu is at the right end of the menu bar, and the Macro functions are listed under the index. In the Macintosh environment, online help is available only if you've clicked on the *Excel* Help icon when you opened the *Excel* directory. This loads *Excel*, as well as the Help files, which are then accessible under About *Excel* in the list of topics shown when you choose the Apple symbol at the far left of the menu bar.

Excel provides a number of debugging tools to let you spot and fix problems, though they differ somewhat in the two environments.

Testing the Macro

The best way to find out whether your macro has bugs in it is to test it in a variety of situations. For instance, if it's going to be run in a network environment, you'll want to verify that it will run correctly both in stand-alone situations and in situations where more than one user is using it. Is it helpful to protect any of the cells? If so, what happens to the logic if they're protected? If they are unprotected?

Will the macro run correctly only in one place on a worksheet? What happens if it writes over existing data?

If there are INPUT statements, what happens if the user enters the wrong type of data? Are the error handling routines sufficient to deal with the kinds of errors that may happen?

At decision points, are all the possible choices covered? For instance, suppose you're comparing a value to 0. If the value is less than 0, the macro does one thing, and if the value is more than 0, the macro does another thing—but what happens if the value is 0?

It's a good idea to make a list of all the conditions that might affect how your macro runs, and test the macro under each condition, one at a time. If appropriate you might also test the macro under some combinations of these conditions, too.

Once you've tested your macro and fixed everything you can find, a good last step is to test it on someone who is unfamiliar with the program, and is close in ability to the kind of person who is likely to be the ultimate user. This person isn't likely to make the same assumptions you do. Pay attention to what this person does, and the questions he asks. If he doesn't know what he's supposed to do next, or if he does something wrong, chances are you need to change something in your approach.

The common phrase for this is *idiot-proofing* your program, but that's a derogatory way of looking at people who just don't see things the way you do, and don't make the same assumptions you do. A good program is one that will run no matter what the biases of the programmer. Check out your assumptions. Verify that you can assume your user knows what you think he knows.

Debugging in the IBM Environment

Excel for the IBM environment contains a Debugger Macro in the Library directory, called DEBUG.XLM. This macro constructs a special environment in which you can test, debug, and run macros. However, Microsoft has supplied no documentation about how this macro runs, other than a short description in the Help file. If you are a paid subscriber to the Microsoft bulletin board system *Online*, there is a bit of documentation about the Debug-

ger there. The results we determined by actually running the Debugger follow in this section.

The Debug macro lets you set breakpoints and tracepoints to
help you pinpoint problems when the macro is running. The Debug macro is located on the Library directory, and must be
opened like any other file. Document protection, however, must
be *off* in order to enter Debug mode. When initially loaded, nothing will appear to be different on your screen, but if you select
the Macro menu, you'll see the Debug. . . command at the bottom of the list of commands.

When you choose the Debug. . . command, you enter the
Debug environment, complete with a new set of menus, grouped
under the menu items Debug, Formula, and Display.

This Debug mode lets you place *breakpoints* and *tracepoints* in
your program. Any changes to your instructions made by the Debugger (such as the addition of breakpoints) are temporary; you
can, however, make permanent changes to your instructions if
you want.

The Debug menu lists several commands (shown in Figure
7-1).

Figure 7-1. Debug Menu Commands

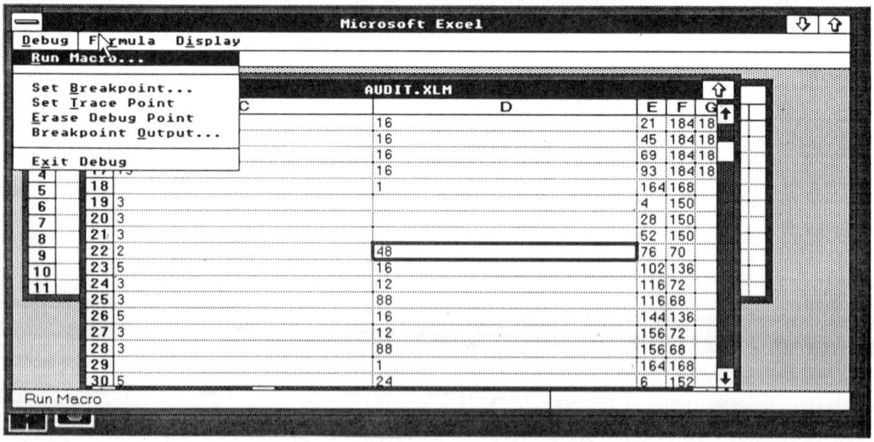

We'll look at running your macro after we've discussed
breakpoints and tracepoints.

Breakpoints. A breakpoint is a point where you want macro execution to stop, at least temporarily. Use the Set Breakpoint command on the Debug menu as shown above. With this command, you tell the macro to halt in the cell where you placed a breakpoint. You can also append a message to your breakpoint that will be displayed in an Alert box when the macro gets to this breakpoint.

Why use a breakpoint? Many complex macros have several ways of handling data, depending on the outcome of certain tests. When a macro fails at some point, it can be very difficult to figure out which logical paths were taken to get to the point of failure. Setting a breakpoint allows you to stop macro execution at points where you're still sure of what paths have been taken.

When a breakpoint is encountered, *Excel* stops macro execution, and displays the value in the cell where it has stopped. You can request more information with the Breakpoint Output command, selected before running the macro. The dialog box presented at this point lets you choose whether to continue, single-step through the rest of the macro, or halt execution.

Tracepoints. A tracepoint is used to let you switch from normal execution of a macro to *single-stepping*. Single-stepping lets you execute the macro's instructions one at a time, usually with a display of associated information (what shows up when you request the Show Info command). Single-stepping is particularly useful for tracing precedents and dependents so you can see how a particular value was derived.

Using breakpoints and tracepoints. Setting a breakpoint or a tracepoint temporarily alters the formula in the cell in which it is located, changing it to an IF statement that has the original formula as one of the arguments. However, the value in that cell is displayed accurately. Notice the breakpoint we inserted in row 6 in the macro in Figure 7-2.

Within Debug mode, you can edit macro statements, or even switch windows, just as you could in a normal operating environment. However, you may not edit the contents of a cell in which a breakpoint or tracepoint has been set.

Let's try this with some files that came with your *Excel* package, to demonstrate how the Debug macro works.

With a blank worksheet on your screen, choose the File Open command, and choose the Library directory. With this directory selected, choose the CALENDAR.XLM macro, and open it. This

Figure 7-2. Formula with Breakpoint

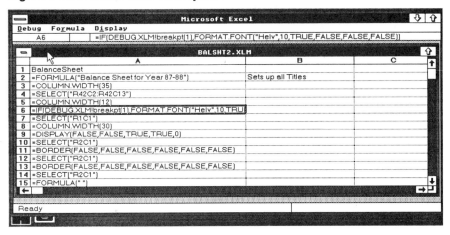

macro creates a printable calendar for the current year, adding holidays in the right days. We'll use this to illustrate how break-points and tracepoints work.

The CALENDAR.XLM macro looks like Figure 7-3 on your screen.

Yes, it's a tiny window. To see more of the macro, use the Control menu to change the size of the window. You can also use the angle-brace in the bottom right corner of the window to *pull* the window into a larger shape. Size the window so it's comfortable for you to see.

Figure 7-3. Calendar Macro

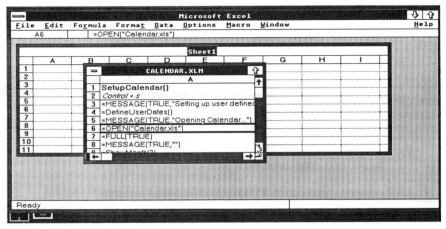

Now open the DEBUG.XLM macro, also in the Library directory. Notice that nothing changes on your screen. However, pull down the Macro menu. You'll find the Debug. . . command at the bottom of the list. When you choose this command, the menu bar changes to show the selections available in Debug mode (Figure 7-4).

Figure 7-4. Debug Menu Bar

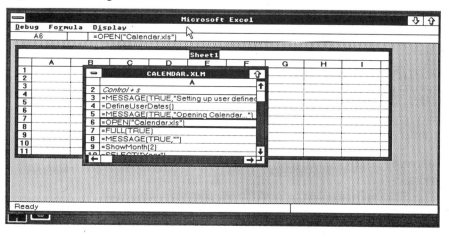

Move the active cell down to row 6, the one with the macro statement =OPEN("Calendar.xls"), and choose the Set Breakpoint command on the Debug menu. The Breakpoint dialog box appears, asking you to type an Alert String (Figure 7-5).

Figure 7-5. Breakpoint Dialog Box

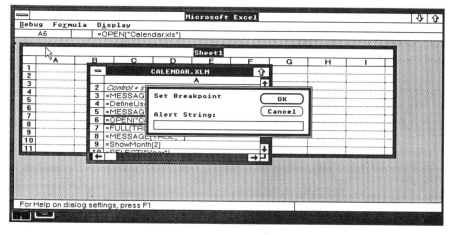

The string *Getting Calendar File* was entered in row 6. When the macro is run in Debug mode and it gets to this instruction, macro execution will halt, and what was typed will appear in an Alert box.

When you choose the OK button, you'll see that Debug changes the instruction in line 6. It now reads:

=IF(DEBUG.XLM!breakpt(1),OPEN("Calendar.xls"))

This is how the Calendar macro will remain as long as you're in Debug mode. When you leave Debug mode, the instruction will be changed back to its original form.

If, when this breakpoint was encountered, you wanted to see the value of a variable in this cell, or see the contents of the cell, you could choose the Breakpoint Output. . . command. Enter the name of the variable or cell reference you want to see in the box that appears.

Now let's insert a tracepoint. Move the active cell down to row 14 and on the Debug menu choose the Set Tracepoint. Notice that the formula in row 14 changes to this:

=IF(STEP( ),MESSAGE(True,"Clearing out old holidays. . ."))

The difference between a breakpoint and a tracepoint. The difference between a breakpoint and a tracepoint is that you're given different information when each is encountered. You'll see how as soon as the macro is run in its new form.

Choose the Run Macro command on the Debug menu. When you're shown the list of available macros, choose *CALENDAR.XLM!Setup.Calendar*. This begins execution of the Setup macro, one of four on the CALENDAR.XLM macro sheet.

In this case, before *Excel* gets to the first breakpoint, you'll hear a tone (depending on your machine, this may be anything from a short chirp to louder beep), and see a series of input boxes, asking if you want to enter your own holidays. If you respond that you want to enter your own holidays, you will be prompted for the month, date, and name. Enter your own holidays (your birthday, for example). Once you've done this, the macro will attempt to execute more instructions. And it will run into the first breakpoint, in row 6. When it does this you'll see the dialog box in Figure 7-6.

Figure 7-6. Breakpoint Dialog Box

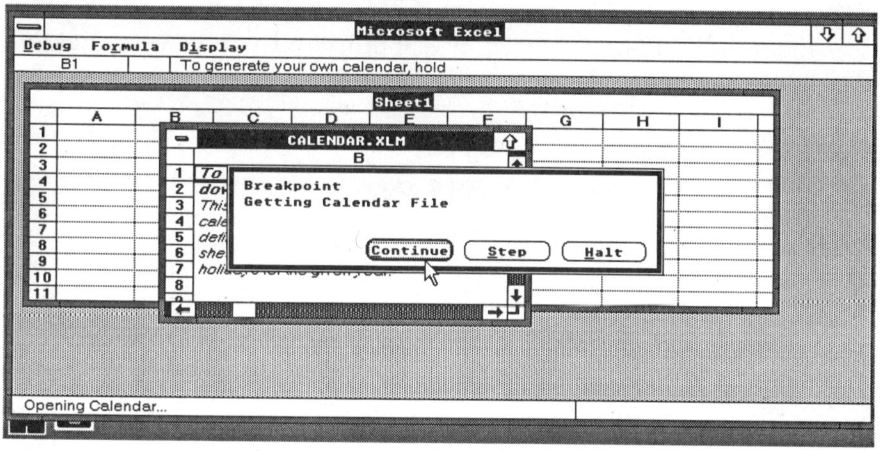

Notice that what you typed as the Alert string now appears as the message in the box.

If you choose the Continue button, macro execution will continue. If you choose the Step button, you'll single-step through the rest of the macro. If you choose the Halt button, execution will stop completely.

For this example, you'll want to continue execution, so choose the Continue button. The macro will set up the calendar in a grid form, by retrieving the CALENDAR.XLS file from the Library directory. You'll see part of it (Figure 7-7).

Figure 7-7. Calendar

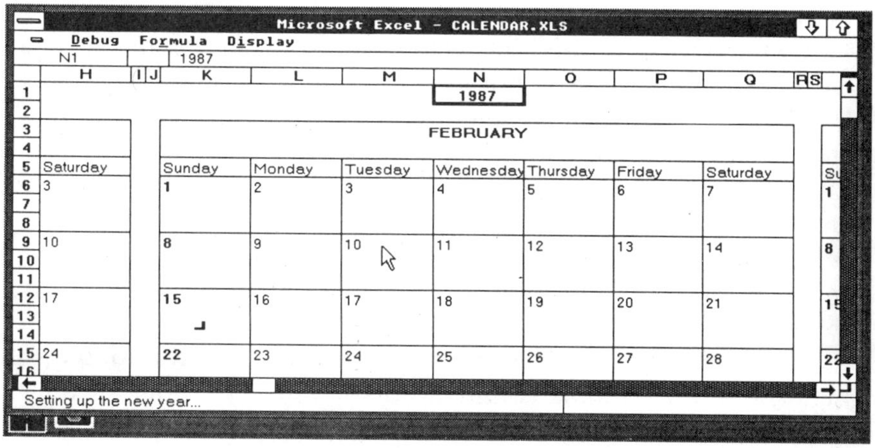

One of the instructions prompts you for the new year. Enter the year for which you wish to generate a calendar.

Eventually, macro execution will stop and you'll see a dialog box in a corner of your screen (Figure 7-8).

Figure 7-8. The Single-Step Dialog Box

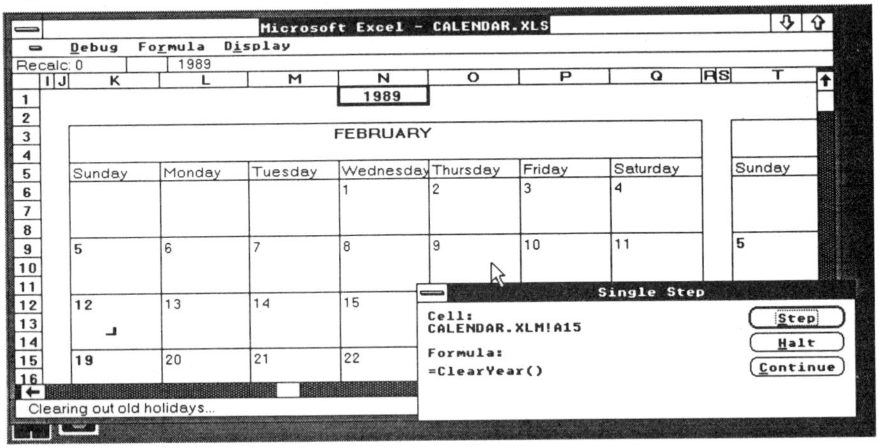

This box, typical of the boxes used with tracepoints, tells you which cell the tracepoint is in, and what the cell contains (in this case, the formula). It also offers you the Step, Halt, and Continue options you had with a breakpoint.

Most people will choose the Step option since the purpose of a tracepoint is to allow you to watch execution of each macro step very carefully. Each time you choose this button, the macro will proceed to the next statement, execute it, and display the same kind of information in the dialog box.

When you've finished inspecting this part of your macro, you can either halt the macro entirely, or continue normal execution.

While you're in the Debug environment, you can also use some other debugging tools. The Display menu lets you choose whether you want formulas or values displayed when your macro runs, and lets you use the Arrange All or Show Info commands on what's currently displayed. The latter two commands work the same way as their equivalent worksheet commands on the Window menu.

The Formula menu lists several more tools useful in debugging. The Show Formula command displays the formula for the active cell in a dialog box. You can select all cells with breakpoints or tracepoints with the Select Debug Points command. You can select all formula cells containing errors with the Select Errors command. You can also use the Note, Goto, and Find commands as you would use them in a worksheet environment.

The Note command is particularly useful in debugging. It works the same in the debugging environment as it does for a normal worksheet or macro sheet. The Note command lets you append text notes to any cell, and in the debugging environment that comes in particularly handy to remind yourself what has happened up to this point.

If you find that you've used the wrong cell name or cell reference in one of your macro statements, it's easy to find the name you want with the Goto command. This lists all defined names in the macro sheet, and asks you to select from the list or give the address of the cell reference you want to use. The Goto finds the cell, makes it the active cell, and displays it on the screen.

The Find. . . command shows a dialog box in which you are to enter the text or value you want to find. You can specify that the search is to be of formulas, values, or notes, you can ask for an exact match or a substring, or you can ask that searching be done by rows or columns if that will make the search process more efficient.

The Run Macro command begins execution of the macro program you choose. If there are no errors in the program, you see nothing further. If there are errors, and breakpoints or tracepoints have been set, macro execution will stop at the first occurrence of a breakpoint or tracepoint, or halt when an error forces it to.

Don't choose the Run Macro command until after you've set any breakpoints or tracepoints you want, since they can't be set once the macro is running in Debug mode. (You can, however, edit the macro to include BREAK statements, but unlike Debug mode these commands will stay with the macro until you take them out.)

Entering the Debug environment will not have any permanent effect on the macro sheet. Cells containing formulas that show a breakpoint or tracepoint in Debug mode will be changed back to their pre-Debug state upon exiting Debug mode. While Debug mode will change the formula in a cell to accommodate a breakpoint or tracepoint, the value resulting from that formula will be the same as before. When you leave Debug mode, the macro sheet cells will all be locked and not hidden.

You can also use some of the debugging facilities without actually being in Debug mode. The macro commands STEP and BREAK can be manually inserted into your macro; the BREAK command is equivalent to inserting a breakpoint as discussed in the section above, and the STEP command causes the macro being run to go into single-step mode, complete with dialog box displays as discussed above.

There are a few other tricks useful to know when you're trying to debug a macro.

- Stop the macro while it's running by pressing the Esc key. This immediately interrupts macro execution and causes a dialog box to be displayed (Figure 7-9).

Figure 7-9. Escape Dialog Box

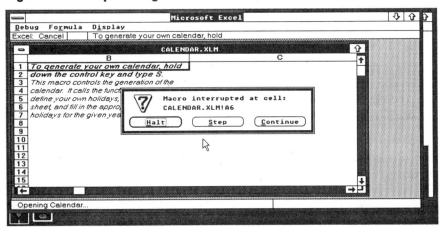

- Halt, Step, and Continue work as described earlier. This method of interrupting execution is most useful when you're running the macro at normal speed (not in Single-Step mode), and find that your macro is doing something you don't like.
- If you've built your macro in small modules, you may wish to add RETURN or HALT instructions at the end of each module while you're debugging. This will mean that as each module executes, it will either return to the known, working part of the program (if the RETURN command is used), or stop as soon as the HALT command is encountered. You can then inspect the values created by the module and see if it worked properly.

144

- Use the windowing ability of *Excel* to run parallel versions of the macro in side-by-side windows. Open two windows, and in one, choose the Formula checkbox under the Options Display command; in the other, leave the Formula checkbox off (which means that values will be displayed). Make sure the windows are sized so you can see what's happening. Open the macro in both windows, and run it simultaneously. You can interrupt the macro at any time to check on the results (Figure 7-10).

Figure 7-10. Debugging with Parallel Windows

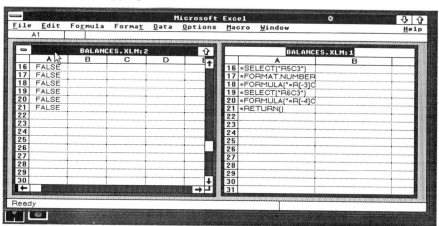

- In the above example, the left window shows values, while formulas appear in the right window. When a macro runs, most of the commands return a TRUE value if the command is executed successfully, or a FALSE value if it isn't. In the example above, the formula in row 18 couldn't be calculated correctly, so an error value was reported.

When you've completed debugging your macro, be sure to edit any extra STEP, BREAK, RETURN, or HALT instructions you inserted.

Debugging in the Macintosh Environment

Version 1.5 of *Excel*, the current version for the Macintosh, doesn't contain a separate debugging facility. That doesn't mean you can't debug what you've written, but it does mean that some of the automatic facilities of the debugger aren't available to you.

However, there are signs that version 2.0 of *Excel* for the Macintosh will contain a debugger similar to the one for the IBM environment.

Debugging in the Macintosh environment requires that you insert the STEP, BREAK, HALT, or RETURN instructions where you want normal running interrupted in a macro that needs debugging. These commands work the same in a Macintosh environment as they do in the IBM environment. You'll want to read the comments above in the section *Debugging in the IBM Environment*.

You can also interrupt execution with the Esc key on the Macintosh the same way this process works in the IBM environment. The box displayed will be approximately the same in both environments.

Because you can't depend on the insertion of breakpoints or tracepoints to bring up an Alert message, it may help you to also insert ALERT commands of your own into the macro just ahead of any RETURN or HALT instructions, while you're still debugging. This will help you track what's going on when the macro stops. You can delete these messages when your macro is working as it should.

Summary

This chapter has shown you how to test and debug your macros in both the IBM and Macintosh environments. It has discussed the process of testing, and shown you how to use breakpoints and tracepoints, as well as some other macro commands that are particularly useful during the debugging process.

Chapter 8
Advanced Macro Topics

This chapter will attempt to explain some of the more advanced topics associated with programming and using *Excel* macros. The concepts we'll discuss aren't all that difficult, but they should be implemented after you've become comfortable with how macros work in general.

Excel's macro language is very powerful; in some ways it's on a par with some of the structured languages like Pascal and C. It lets you open and close external files, parse individual records to extract information at a specific location, test for the presence of certain data and pass control to other macros, and use arrays to help deal with sets of data.

However, it should be noted that *Excel's* macro language is not as comprehensive as these other programming languages. It was never intended to be. It is, however, designed to help you, the business user, take full advantage of the functions within *Excel* to streamline and automate some of your business problem-solving activities.

Automatic Macros

You've probably seen AUTOEXEC.BAT files in an IBM environment. They're used to do certain things automatically when the computer is turned on. Among other things, these files can display the time and date, initialize some background utility files, set up a screen capture facility, or specify what your onscreen prompt is to look like. In the Macintosh environment, you may have seen files like this created with the *MacroMaker,* a utility normally stored with the System Folder, or other files that are stored for startup purposes, such as the sound and color files.

You can set up macros in *Excel* so they'll run automatically whenever you open or close a given document, choose a particular key or command, encounter an error or interrupt condition, or change data linked to another document.

Be sure any macro you want to run automatically is completely debugged, or you might discover that its running actually *causes* more errors in other macro programs.

In *Excel*, an automatic macro is always linked to a particular document. To specify that a macro is to be run automatically, open the document, and choose the Formula Define Name. In the Name box, type

Auto_open

and in the Refers To box, type the reference (name or starting address, as you prefer) of the macro you want to run automatically. Then choose the OK button.

From then on, when you open this document, the macro will run automatically. If you entered an external reference in the Refers To box when you defined the macro, *Excel* opens the macro sheet involved and then runs the macro.

You can also specify that a macro is to be run automatically whenever a document is closed. The procedure is the same as for running a macro when a document is opened, except that to specify closing, you type

Auto_close

in the Name box.

You can use an "autoexec" macro to load a specified set of files automatically every time you start *Excel*. Here's an autoexec macro that automatically loads the files necessary to link the annual budget with the monthly income statement for both the current and previous months.

This example was presented in more detail in our companion book *PC Excel Business Solutions*. The files are linked so figures from the previous month's file can be used to compute running totals for the year, and figures from the annual budget can be compared with actual figures for the month. The macro loads them all, letting you specify which month's budget you want to work on, and automatically retrieving the previous month's budget and the annual budget.

You can also use autoexec macros to create demonstration programs, or for situations where you want to have the computer

Figure 8-1. "Autoexec" Macro to Load Files

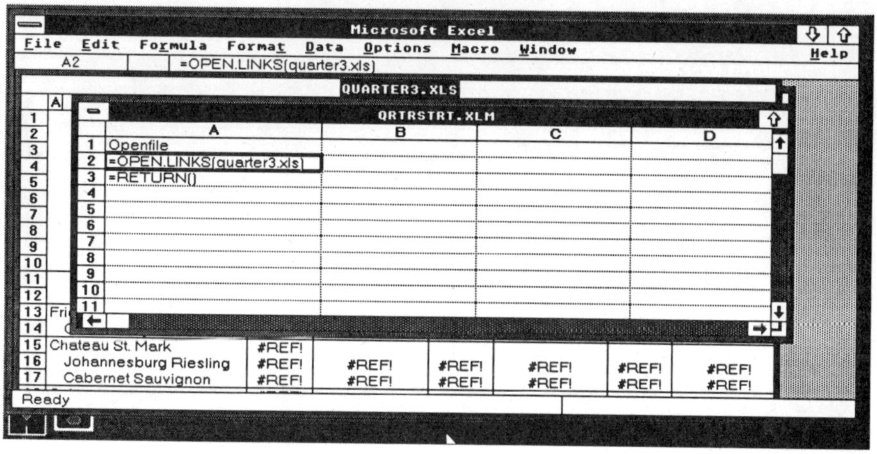

make a presentation for you. Such a demo might open a file containing numbers, and translate those numbers into a graph, displaying information about the numbers in a note that's displayed on the screen as the user watches.

Use ALERT and MESSAGE commands to display some kinds of messages, or use the DISPLAY command to show the contents of notes attached to selected cells.

Probably the easiest way to make a demo macro that runs automatically is to use the Recorder to translate your steps into macro commands. Edit the result, making sure the reader will have time to read what's on the screen. (The WAIT function lets you essentially freeze what's on the screen for a specified period of time, then resume macro execution.)

Once you've gotten your demo to run, look it over for eye appeal. You may make it easier to see by turning off the gridlines, or using borders or shading for emphasis, or by selecting bigger or different typefaces.

Here's a demo macro that translates a series of expense figures to a pie chart with explanations.

Figure 8-2. Demo Macro

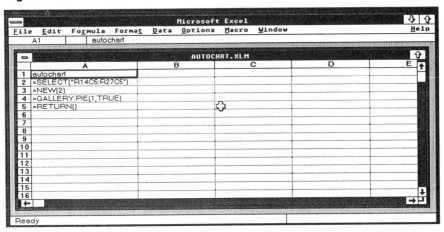

Figure 8-3. Chart Produced by Macro

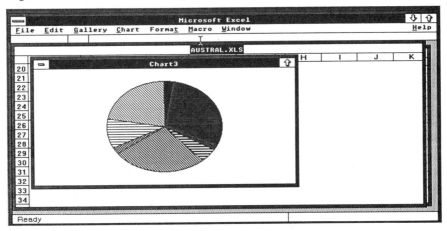

Notice that the note displayed above is only one of several in the macro. The macro cycles through the display of several explanatory notes, pausing between each so the user has time to read them.

If you're using *Microsoft Windows* (version 2.0 or higher) in the IBM environment, you can also execute other programs, and exchange information with other *Windows* applications, such as other spreadsheet, database, or text files.

To start another *Windows* application, use the EXEC macro function, as described in Appendix B. To start a procedure in a *Windows* library, use the CALL and REGISTER macro functions.

Creating Custom Menus and Dialog Boxes

What is referred to as the MENU function in other spreadsheets is covered in both *Excel* for the IBM environment and *Excel* for the Macintosh environment by the Macro Run command. Other programs' MENU functions bring up the equivalent of a dialog box, listing the macros available, and sometimes providing a comment about each of them. With either version of *Excel*, you must first open a macro sheet, but when you choose the Macro Run command, you'll see the equivalent of all named macros on the current sheet.

Excel goes a step further. You can create your own custom menus and dialog boxes with several macro functions. The following commands are involved with menu bars, menus, and commands:

ADD.BAR
ADD.COMMAND
ADD.MENU
CHECK.COMMAND
DELETE.BAR
DELETE.COMMAND
DELETE.MENU
GET.BAR
ENABLE.COMMAND
RENAME.COMMAND
SHOW.BAR

The only command involved with custom dialog boxes is the DIALOG.BOX command. (The ALERT command displays one of *Excel*'s simple dialog boxes, and the INPUT command displays a simple dialog box with text that you specify.)

Custom menu bars are particularly useful if you have special applications that need to run macros, accessed by direct commands rather than through the Macro Run commands.

Custom menu bars are discussed in detail in the section *Custom Menus and Dialog Boxes* in Chapter 6 of the *Functions and Macros* reference manual for *Excel* in the IBM environment, and in Chapter 8 of the *Arrays, Functions, and Macros* reference manual for *Excel* in the Macintosh environment.

Custom dialog boxes are particularly useful if you're trying to create a macro that requires the user to enter a variety of data, but where you need to control what is entered. Figure 8-4 shows

151

a custom dialog box used to control entry of information about students and their homeroom assignments.

Figure 8-4. Custom Dialog Box, Student Data

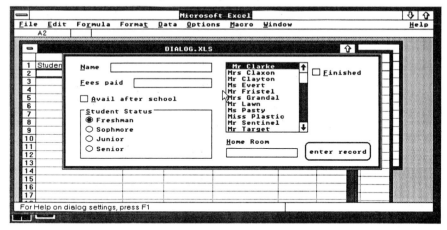

The macro that creates this box doesn't look like an ordinary macro. The DIALOG.BOX command refers to an area that describes your dialog box, in a table that looks like Figure 8-5.

Setting up a custom dialog box is a very complex operation, and is described in detail in the same section of the reference manual in which custom menus is described. Rather than repeat what's in the manual, we suggest you look there.

Figure 8-5. Table for Student Data Custom Dialog Box

	A	B	C	D	E	F	G
1	Student Name	Fees Paid	After School	Student standing	Home Room		
2	Robert Adams	1220	FALSE	Freshman	0		
3	Tobin Brocket	950	TRUE	Senior	Mr. Sentinel		
4	Charles Cala	1220	TRUE	Senior	Mr. Target		
5	Better Davis	850	FALSE	Junior	Mr. Target		
6	Adolf Eichman	650	TRUE	Freshman	Mr. Fristel		
7	Ray Feist	850	FALSE	Junior	Ms. Pasty		
8	Jerry Gemini	850	TRUE	Sophomore	Miss Grunhilde		
9	Hedda Hopeful	500	TRUE	Junior	Mr. Target		
10	Iris Instep	850	TRUE	Sophomore	Mr. Clarke		
11	Jeremy Jouge	850	FALSE	Senior	Mr. Falcon		
12	Larry Liuzardo	800	FALSE	Sophomore	Mr. Sentinel		
13	Mary Marple	1750	TRUE	Junior	Mr. Lawn		
14	Nancy Nice	1750	FALSE	Freshman	Mr. Clayton		
15							
16							

Protecting Program Logic

Excel gives you several ways of protecting your data and formulas from accidental alteration. This is particularly important if your macro sets up a template and uses input that's not specifically prompted for (with an INPUT box) and checked for accuracy.

You can reduce the danger that a macro can be tampered with by restricting input to INPUT boxes, or the use of custom menus and dialog boxes.

The Protect Document command on the Options menu lets you specify a password so only those who know the password can open your macro. This prevents anyone who isn't authorized from being able to use your macro.

One major failing of password protection is that people tend to let others know the password. To prevent this, you should make sure everyone knows and understands the reason for password protection, and that the reason is accepted by all.

Another failing is that human beings forget, and forgetting a password is a fairly common occurrence. If you protect yourself against forgetting the password by storing a copy of the password in a safe place, not only could someone else stumble across the password, but you might forget where the safe place is. Think long and hard about using passwords to protect your macros.

You can also protect your macro by hiding or locking cells. You can do this with the Cell Protection command on the Format menu. On a selected cell basis, you can:

• Lock the cell so it can't be altered.
• Hide it, so only the *contents* will be visible on the macro sheet, but the *formula* won't appear in the formula bar.

Neither of these commands take effect until you choose the Protect Document command on the Options menu.

An undocumented method of hiding numeric values in cells is to use the Blank Cell format, available with the Format Number command. (This method works with both the IBM and Macintosh versions of *Excel*.) It doesn't appear as an option when you inspect the list of available options. However, it hides the numeric (but not text) values of the cells selected. It also hides the values resulting from a formula in a selected cell.

To use this method, type the values you want, then select the cells they're in. Next, choose the Format Number command, press Backspace or Delete, type a space, and press Enter (or Return on the Macintosh). This chooses the Blank Number format that now appears as an option on the Format menu. The result is a blank line, which is selected. Press Enter again, if necessary.

Figure 8-6. Cell Blank Option, Format Number Command

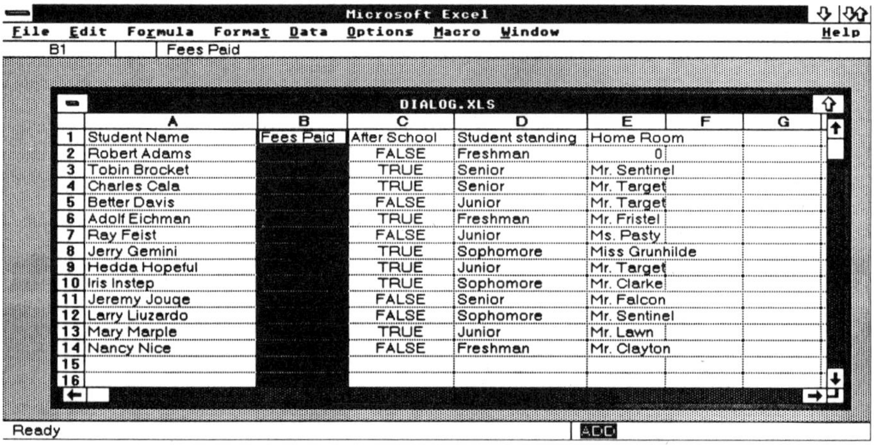

The numeric values disappear from the selected cells on the worksheet; however, each appears in the formula bar when the cell is selected, much the way the Hide command works.

Note that this format doesn't work with text. It only works with numeric values. If the formula producing a value is evaluated as a negative value, you'll see a minus sign in the selected cell on the worksheet, but not the rest of the number.

Once you've used this procedure to invoke the Cell Blank option on the Format Number command, you can use this option anywhere else on your macro sheet or worksheet.

Another way to protect data is to use the Column Width and Row Height commands in the IBM environment, or the Column Width command in the Macintosh environment. If the column width or row height is set to 0, the column disappears from the screen. Any data in any cell in that column disappears also. The cell can still be referenced by other cells, and the data in that cell can be altered by the actions of formulas, but it isn't visible.

This technique is particularly useful when your macro sheet

contains a set of instructions you don't particularly want a user to see, but when the instructions need to be on an open sheet.

The IBM environment offers yet another way to protect your macro sheet. The Hide command on the Window menu lets you hide an entire macro sheet, much as the Hide command on the Options menu lets you hide cells. When you hide a window containing a macro sheet, you don't see the macro but you can still access it by documents having external references to the macros on the hidden window.

Two more macro commands are available for the IBM environment, which let you prevent users from stopping a macro while it's running (CANCEL.KEY) and stop all user input except responses to dialog boxes (DISABLE.INPUT).

Using Arrays

Arrays are groups of numbers that can be handled as a unit. *Excel* uses two types of arrays:

- Array ranges are used with formulas that can produce multiple results.
- Array constants are used as arguments in a formula.

When you use an array in a formula, you identify this by enclosing the formula in braces:

{=HOUR(C5:C15)}

An array formula using an array range is usually placed in one cell, but is evaluated so its results are placed in cells that fill out the rectangle (Figure 8-7).

You enter an array formula by pressing a special set of keys:

- In the IBM environment, select the range. Then enter the formula, and press Ctrl-Shift-Enter. *Excel* places the formula in each of the cells indicated as the array range.
- In the Macintosh environment, select the range, then enter the formula, and press Command-Return. The array is placed in the array range.

Figure 8-7. Formula Using Array Range

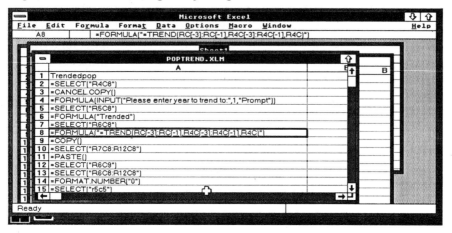

If you place an array formula in a single cell rather than a range, you'll get the sum of the results of the formula applied to the cells specified. The formula

$$\{ = SUM(A5:A7*E5:E7)\}$$

placed in a single cell is evaluated as

$$(A5*E5) + (A6*E6) + (A7*E7)$$

while the result if placed in the range F5:F7 is

```
    F
5  A5*E5
6  A6*E6
7  A7*E7
```

Editing an array is a bit different from editing a regular worksheet formula because the array range shares one formula, even though it appears in each cell of the array. Select the array range, then edit the single formula that appears. Be sure to press Ctrl-Shift-Enter in the IBM environment, or press the Command key when you enter the edited formula. Otherwise, you'll replace the array formula with a normal formula.

Some editing operations can't be performed on an array. You can't clear, move, delete, or change the contents of only one portion of the array, nor can you insert cells within the array range. You have to make changes that affect the array as a whole.

Array constants are used instead of single values in an argument. For example, the TREND function lets you pick the month for which you want a trended value, based on values for prior periods. Suppose you have a set of birth figures for the last five years, and you'd like an estimate of births for the next three years. In the example below, the formula

=TREND(B4:B8,,{6,7,8})

evaluates the birth figures in B4 through B8, and using a linear trending model projects the figures for the sixth, seventh, and eighth years (Figure 8-8).

Figure 8-8. Trended Figures Using an Array Constant

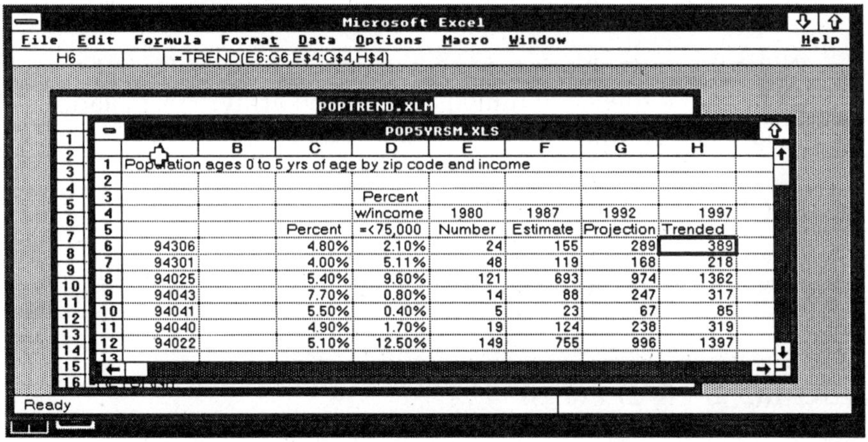

You can use one-dimensional arrays or two-dimensional arrays as array constants. The following are one-dimensional arrays:

To Get	Type
50 75 100 125 150	{50,75,100,125,150}*
10	{10;20;30;40;50}*
20	
30	
40	
50	

*Notice that commas are used to separate values in a horizontal array, but semicolons are used to separate values in a vertical array.

The following is a two-dimensional array:

To Get	Type
1 2 3 4	{1,2,3,4;233,248,257,262}
233 248 257 262	

When you use an array as an argument, be sure the other arguments have the same dimensions as the array. For instance, if you have the formula

=SUM({2,4,6}*2)

Excel assumes that the second argument, 2, will be used three times:

=SUM((2*2)+(4*2)+(6*2)) = 24

If the dimensions of the array in the formula and the array where the results are to be displayed aren't the same, you may get an error message.

Arrays are discussed in more detail in the *Microsoft Excel Reference Guide*, which comes with the software.

Using Text Files

Your macros can work with text (ASCII) files, as well as with data files. Any text file you use must be opened and closed, but it can be inspected and read, either wholly or partially. You can also write information from *Excel*, as text, into the text file.

Use FOPEN and FCLOSE to open and close a text file. If successful, FOPEN returns a document number, which you can then use to refer to the file with the other file manipulation macro commands. FSIZE lets you determine the size of the file, and PARSE lets you distribute data according to an algorithm you choose.

FPOS lets you position the read or write entry point at a specific number of bytes from the beginning of the file. FREAD lets you read a specific number of characters from the file you specify, and FREADLN lets you read a string of characters, ending with the first Carriage Return/Line Feed character pair. FWRITE lets you write whatever you specify, as text, into the file, and FWRITELN lets you write the text as a line, along with a Carriage Return/Line Feed character pair.

Summary

This chapter has given you a brief look at some advanced macro techniques available within *Excel*. We've looked at creating and using macros that execute automatically, use custom menus and dialog boxes, protect your program logic, use arrays, and pass information to and from text files. This chapter has given you a brief overview of these topics, but we suggest you look at the *Excel* reference manuals for more detailed explanations.

Appendix A
Quick Reference Guide
Excel for the IBM Environment

Menus
Worksheet Menus

File menu

New. . .
Open. . .
Close
Save
Save As. . .
Page Setup. . .
Print. . .
Printer Setup. . .
Exit

Edit menu

Undo
Repeat
Cut
Copy
Paste
Clear. . .
Paste Special. . .
Paste Link. . .
Delete. . .
Insert. . .

160

Fill Right
Fill Down

Formula menu

Paste Name. . .
Paste Function. . .
Reference
Define Name. . .
Create Name. . .
Apply Names. . .
Note. . .
Goto. . .
Find. . .
Replace. . .
Select Special. . .

Format menu

Number. . .
Alignment. . .
Font. . .
Border. . .
Cell Protection. . .
Row Height. . .
Column Width. . .
Justify

Data menu

Form. . .
Find
Extract. . .
Delete
Set Database
Set Criteria
Sort. . .
Series. . .
Table. . .
Parse. . .

Options menu

Set Print Area
Set Print Titles
Set Page Break
Display. . .
Freeze Panes
Protect Document. . .
Calculation. . .
Calculate Now
Workspace. . .
Short Menus

Macro menu

Record. . .
Run. . .
Start Recorder
Set Recorder
Relative Record

Window menu

New Window
Show Info
Arrange All
Hide
Unhide
1 Sheet1.XLS

Help menu

Index
Keyboard
Lotus 123. . .
Multiplan. . .
Tutorial
Feature Guide
About. . .

Chart Menus
File menu

New. . .

Open. . .

Close

Save. . .

Save As. . .

Save Workspace. . .

Delete. . .

Page Setup. . .

Print. . .

Printer Setup. . .

Exit

Edit menu

Undo

Repeat

Cut

Copy

Paste

Clear. . .

Paste Special. . .

Gallery menu

Area. . .

Bar. . .

Column. . .

Line. . .

Pie. . .

Scatter. . .

Combination. . .

Preferred

Set Preferred

Chart menu

Attach Text. . .

Add Arrow

Add Legend

Axes
Gridlines. . .
Add Overlay
Select Chart
Select Plot Area
Protect Document
Calculate Now
Short Menus

Format menu

Patterns. . .
Font. . .
Text. . .
Scale. . .
Legend. . .
Main Chart. . .
Overlay. . .
Move
Size

Macro menu

Record. . .
Run. . .
Start Recorder

Window menu

Arrange All
Hide
Unhide
1 Chart1.XLC

Help menu

Index
Keyboard
Lotus 123. . .
Multiplan. . .
Tutorial
Feature Guide
About. . .

Info Window Menus

File menu

New. . .
Open. . .
Close
Save. . .
Save As. . .
Save Workspace. . .
Delete. . .
Page Setup. . .
Print. . .
Printer Setup. . .
Exit

Info menu

Cell
Formula
Value
Format
Protection
Names
Precedents
Dependents
Note

Macro menu

Record. . .
Run. . .
Start Recorder

Window menu

Show Document
Arrange All
Unhide Window
1 Chart1.XLC

Help menu

Index
Keyboard

Lotus 123. . .

Multiplan. . .

Tutorial

Feature Guide

About. . .

Application Control Menu

Restore

Move

Size

Minimize

Maximize

Close

Run. . .

Document Control Menu

Restore

Move

Size

Maximize

Close

Split

Functions

Database Functions

DAVERAGE(*database,field,criteria*)

DCOUNT(*database,field,criteria*)

DCOUNTA(*database,field,criteria*)

DMAX(*database,field,criteria*)

DMIN(*database,field,criteria*)

DPRODUCT(*database,field,criteria*)

DSTDEV(*database,field,criteria*)

DSTDEVP(*database,field,criteria*)

DSUM(*database,field,criteria*)

DVAR(*database,field,criteria*)

DVARP(*database,field,criteria*)

Date and Time Functions

DATE(*year,month,day*)
DATEVALUE(*date__text*)
DAY(*serial__number*)
HOUR(*serial__number*)
MINUTE(*serial__number*)
MONTH(*serial__number*)
NOW( )
SECOND(*serial__number*)
TIME(*hour,minute,second*)
TIMEVALUE(*time__text*)
WEEKDAY(*serial__number*)
YEAR(*serial__number*)

Financial Functions

DDB(*cost,salvage,life,period*)
FV(*rate,nper,payment,present__value,type*)
IPMT(*rate,period,nper,present__value,future__value,type*)
IRR(*values,guess*)
MIRR(*values,finance__rate,reinvest__rate*)
NPER(*rate,payment,present__value,future__value,type*)
NPV(*rate,value1,value2,. . .*)
PMT(*rate,nper,present__value,future__value,type*)
PPMT(*rate,period,nper,present__value,future__value,type*)
PV(*rate,nper,payment,future__value,type*)
RATE(*nper,payment,present__value,future__value,type,guess*)
SLN(*cost,salvage,life*)
SYD(*cost,salvage,life,period*)

Information Functions

AREAS(*reference*)
CELL(*type__of__info,reference*)
COLUMN(*reference*)
COLUMNS(*array*)
INDIRECT(*reference__text,type__of__reference*)
ISBLANK(*value*)
ISERR(*value*)
ISERROR(*value*)
ISLOGICAL(*value*)
ISNA(*value*)

ISNONTEXT(*value*)
ISNUMBER(*value*)
ISREF(*value*)
ISTEXT(*value*)
N(*value*)
NA( )
ROW(*reference*)
ROWS(*array*)
T(*value*)
TYPE(*value*)

Logical Functions

AND(*logical1,logical2,. . .*)
FALSE( )
IF(*logical__test,value__if__true,value__if__false*)
NOT(*logical*)
OR(*logical1,logical2,. . .*)
TRUE( )

Lookup Functions

CHOOSE(*index__number,value1,value2,. . .*)
HLOOKUP(*lookup__value,table__array,row__index__num*)
INDEX(*array,row__number,column__number*)
LOOKUP(*lookup__value,lookup__vector,result__vector*)
LOOKUP(*lookup__value,array*)
MATCH(*lookup__value,lookup__array,type__of__match*)
VLOOKUP(*lookup__value,table__array,column__index*)

Mathematical Functions

ABS(*number*)
EXP(*number*)
FACT(*number*)
INT(*number*)
LN(*number*)
LOG(*number,base*)
LOG10(*number*)
MOD(*number,divisor__number*)
PI( )
PRODUCT(*number1,number2,. . .*)
RAND( )
ROUND(*number,number__of__digits*)

SIGN(*number*)
SQRT(*number*)
TRUNC(*number*)

Matrix Functions

MDETERM(*array*)
MINVERSE(*array*)
MMULT(*array1,array2*)
TRANSPOSE(*array*)

Statistical Functions

AVERAGE(*number1,number2,. . .*)
COUNT(*value1,value2,. . .*)
COUNTA(*value1,value2,. . .*)
GROWTH(*known__y's,known__x's,new__x's*)
LINEST(*known__y's,known__x's*)
LOGEST(*known__y's,known__x's*)
MAX(*number1,number2,. . .*)
MIN(*number1,number2,. . .*)
STDEV(*number1,number2,. . .*)
STDEVP(*number1,number2,. . .*)
SUM(*number1,number2,. . .*)
TREND(*known__y's,known__x's,new__x's*)
VAR(*number1,number2,. . .*)
VARP(*number1,number2,. . .*)

Text Functions

CHAR(*number*)
CLEAN(*text*)
CODE(*text*)
DOLLAR(*number,decimals*)
EXACT(*text1,text2*)
FIND(*find__text,within__text,start__at__number*)
FIXED(*number,decimals*)
LEFT(*text,number__of__characters*)
LEN(*text*)
LOWER(*text*)
MID(*text,start__number,number__of__characters*)
PROPER(*text*)
REPLACE(*old__text,start__num,num__chars,new__text*)
REPT(*text,number__of__times*)

RIGHT(*text,number__of__chars*)
SEARCH(*find__text,within__text,start__at__num*)
SUBSTITUE(*text,old__text,new__text,instance__number*)
TEXT(*value,format__text*)
TRIM(*text*)
UPPER(*text*)
VALUE(*text*)

Trigonometric Functions

ACOS(*number*)
ASIN(*number*)
ATAN(*number*)
ATAN2(*x__number,y__number*)
COS(*radians*)
SIN(*radians*)
TAN(*radians*)

Command Equivalent Functions

Command	Macro Function
Chart Add Arrow	ADD.ARROW
Chart Add Legend	LEGEND
Chart Add Overlay*	ADD.OVERLAY
Chart Attach Text	ATTACH.TEXT
Chart Axes	AXES
Chart Calculate Document	CALCULATE.DOCUMENT
Chart Calculate Now	CALCULATE.NOW
Chart Delete Arrow	DELETE.ARROW
Chart Delete Legend	LEGEND
Chart Delete Overlay*	DELETE.OVERLAY
Chart Full Menus	SHORT.MENUS
Chart Gridlines	GRIDLINES
Chart Protect Document*	PROTECT.DOCUMENT
Chart Select Chart	SELECT
Chart Select Plot Area	SELECT
Chart Short Menus*	SHORT.MENUS
Chart Unprotect Document*	PROTECT.DOCUMENT

Control Close (application)	QUIT
Control Close (document)	CLOSE
Control Maximize (application)	APP.MAXIMIZE
Control Maximize (document)	FULL
Control Minimize	APP.MINIMIZE
Control Move (application)	APP.MOVE
Control Move (document)	MOVE
Control Restore (application)	APP.RESTORE
Control Restore (document)	FULL
Control Run	no equivalent
Control Size (application)	APP.SIZE
Control Size (document)	SIZE
Control Split	SPLIT
Data Delete*	DATA.DELETE
Data Exit Find	DATA.FIND
Data Extract*	EXTRACT
Data Find	DATA.FIND
Data Form	DATA.FORM
Data Parse*	PARSE
Data Series	DATA.SERIES
Data Set Criteria	SET.CRITERIA
Data Set Database	SET.DATABASE
Data Sort	SORT
Data Table*	TABLE
Edit Clear	CLEAR
Edit Copy	COPY
Edit Copy Picture	COPY.PICTURE
Edit Cut	CUT
Edit Delete	EDIT.DELETE
Edit Fill Down	FILL.DOWN
Edit Fill Left	FILL.LEFT
Edit Fill Right	FILL.RIGHT
Edit Fill Up	FILL.UP
Edit Insert	INSERT
Edit Paste	PASTE

Edit Paste Link*	PASTE.LINK
Edit Paste Special*	PASTE.SPECIAL
Edit Repeat*	no equivalent
Edit Undo	UNDO
File Close	FILE.CLOSE
File Close All	CLOSE.ALL
File Delete*	FILE.DELETE
File Exit	QUIT
File Links*	OPEN.LINKS or CHANGE.LINKS
File New	NEW
File Open	OPEN
File Page Setup	PAGE.SETUP
File Print	PRINT
File Printer Setup	PRINTER.SETUP
File Record Macro	no equivalent
File Save	SAVE
File Save As	SAVE.AS
File Save Workspace*	SAVE.WORKSPACE
File Unhide Window	UNHIDE
Format Alignment	ALIGNMENT
Format Border	BORDER
Format Cell Protection*	CELL.PROTECTION
Format Column Width	COLUMN.WIDTH
Format Font	FORMAT.FONT and REPLACE.FONT
Format Justify*	JUSTIFY
Format Legend	FORMAT.LEGEND
Format Main Chart	MAIN.CHART
Format Move	FORMAT.MOVE
Format Number	FORMAT.NUMBER
Format Overlay	OVERLAY
Format Patterns	PATTERNS
Format Row Height	ROW.HEIGHT
Format Scale	SCALE
Format Size	FORMAT.SIZE
Format Text	FORMAT.TEXT

Formula Apply Names*	APPLY.NAMES
Formula Create Names	CREATE.NAMES
Formula Define Names	DEFINE.NAMES and DELETE.NAMES
Formula Find	FORMULA.FIND
Formula Goto	FORMULA.GOTO
Formula Note	NOTE
Formula Paste Function	no equivalent
Formula Paste Name	LIST.NAMES
Formula Reference	no equivalent
Formula Replace*	FORMULA.REPLACE
Formula Select Special*	SELECT.SPECIAL
Gallery Area	GALLERY.AREA
Gallery Bar	GALLERY.BAR
Gallery Column	GALLERY.COLUMN
Gallery Combination*	COMBINATION
Gallery Line	GALLERY.LINE
Gallery Pie	GALLERY.PIE
Gallery Preferred*	PREFERRED
Gallery Scatter	GALLERY.SCATTER
Gallery Set Preferred*	SET.PREFERRED
Info Cell	DISPLAY
Info Dependents	DISPLAY
Info Format	DISPLAY
Info Formula	DISPLAY
Info Names	DISPLAY
Info Note	DISPLAY
Info Precedents	DISPLAY
Info Protection	DISPLAY
Info Value	DISPLAY
Macro Absolute Record	no equivalent
Macro Record	no equivalent
Macro Relative Record	no equivalent
Macro Run	RUN
Macro Set Recorder	no equivalent
Macro Start Recorder	no equivalent

Macro Stop Recorder	no equivalent
Options Calculate Document	CALCULATE.DOCUMENT
Options Calculate Now	CALCULATE.NOW
Options Calculation	CALCULATION or PRECISION
Options Display	DISPLAY
Options Freeze Panes	FREEZE.PANES
Options Full Menus	SHORT.MENUS
Options Protect Document*	PROTECT.DOCUMENT
Options Remove Page Break	REMOVE.PAGE.BREAK
Options Set Page Break*	SET.PAGE.BREAK
Options Set Print Area	SET.PRINT.AREA
Options Set Print Titles*	SET.PRINT.TITLES
Options Short Menus*	SHORT.MENUS
Options Unfreeze Panes*	UNFREEZE.PANES
Options Unprotect Document*	PROTECT.DOCUMENT
Options Workspace*	WORKSPACE
Window Document	ACTIVATE
Window Arrange All	ARRANGE.ALL
Window Hide*	HIDE
Window New Window	NEW.WINDOW
Window Show Document*	SHOW.INFO
Window Show Info*	SHOW.INFO
Window Unhide*	UNHIDE

*Full menus

Action Equivalent Functions

Function	Action
A1.R1C1	Displays either the A1 or R1C1 references.
ACTIVATE	Selects a window.
ACTIVATE.NEXT	Selects the next window.
ACTIVATE.PREV	Selects the previous window.
CANCEL.COPY	Cancels the marquee.
COPY.CHART	Copies an image of a chart.
DATA.FIND.NEXT	Finds the next matching record in a database.

DATA.FIND.PREV	Finds the previous matching record in a database.
DELETE.FORMAT	Deletes a Format Number command format.
DIRECTORY	Changes directories and provides a new path name.
FORMULA	Enters either a formula in a cell, or text on a chart.
FORMULA.ARRAY	Enters an array formula on a document.
FORMULA.FILL	Fills a cell range with a formula.
FORMULA.FIND.NEXT	Finds the next cell, as described in the Formula Find dialog box.
FORMULA.FIND.PREV	Finds the previous cell, as described in the Formula Find dialog box.
HLINE	Horizontally scrolls the active window column by column.
HPAGE	Horizontally scrolls the active window one window at a time.
HSCROLL	Horizontally scrolls a document by either a column number or a percentage.
SELECT	Selects an object on a chart.
SELECT	Selects a reference.
SELECT.END	Changes the active cell.
SELECT.LAST.CELL	Selects the cell at the end of the document.
SHOW.ACTIVE.CELL	Displays the currently active cell.
SHOW.CLIPBOARD	Displays the Clipboard.
STYLE	Changes the font being used.
UNLOCKED.NEXT	Jumps to the next unlocked cell.
UNLOCKED.PREV	Jumps to the previous unlocked cell.
VLINE	Scrolls the active window vertically by rows.
VPAGE	Scrolls the active window vertically one window at a time.
VSCROLL	Scrolls the document vertically by either a row number or a percentage.

Customizing Functions

Function	Action
ADD.BAR	Adds a custom menu bar.
ADD.COMAND	Adds a custom command.
ADD.MENU	Adds a custom menu.
ALERT	Displays a dialog box.
APP.ACTIVATE	Starts another program.

BEEP	Causes your computer to emit a beep tone.
CALL	Calls the *Windows* library.
CANCEL.KEY	Alters Esc key.
CHECK.COMMAND	Marks a command.
DELETE.BAR	Removes a custom menu bar.
DELETE.COMMAND	Removes a custom command.
DELETE.MENU	Removes a custom menu.
DIALOG.BOX	Creates a custom dialog box.
DISABLE.INPUT	Stops all input to *Excel.*
ECHO	Turns the screen update on or off.
ENABLE.COMMAND	Enables or disables a custom command.
ERROR	Specifies the action to take if an error occurs while a macro is running.
EXEC	Starts another program.
EXECUTE	Executes a command under another program.
FCLOSE	Closes a text file.
FOPEN	Opens a text file.
FPOS	Returns the current position in a text file.
FREAD	Reads characters from a text file.
FREADLN	Reads a line from a text file.
FSIZE	Returns the size of a text file.
FWRITE	Writes characters to a text file.
FWRITELN	Writes a full line to a text file.
HELP	Displays a Help topic.
INITIATE	Opens a channel to another program.
INPUT	Displays a dialog box.
MESSAGE	Displays a message in the status bar.
ON.DATA	Starts a macro as soon as data is sent to *Excel* by another program.
ON.KEY	Starts a macro as soon as a particular key is pressed.
ON.TIME	Starts a macro at a specified time.
ON.WINDOW	Starts a macro when a specified window is changed.
POKE	Sends data to another program.
REGISTER	Used to access the *Microsoft Windows* library.
RENAME.COMMAND	Renames a command.
REQUEST	Returns data from another program.

SEND.KEYS	Sends a key sequence to another program.
SET.NAME	Sets a name to a certain value.
SET.VALUE	Enters a value in a cell.
SHOW.BAR	Displays a menu bar.
STEP	Steps through a macro.
TERMINATE	Closes a channel to another program.
WAIT	Pauses a macro during its execution.

Control Functions

Function	Action
ARGUMENT	Describes function arguments to a macro.
BREAK	Breaks from a FOR-NEXT or WHILE-NEXT loop.
FOR	Begins a FOR-NEXT loop.
GOTO	Moves to another cell.
HALT	Stops a macro or macros from running.
NEXT	Closing statement of a FOR-NEXT or WHILE-NEXT loop.
RESTART	Removes return addresses from the stack.
RESULT	Specifies the data type of a function macro's return value.
RETURN	Returns control to whatever caused the macro to start.
WHILE	Begins a WHILE-NEXT loop.

Value-Returning Functions

Function	Action
ABSREF	Returns the absolute reference of a cell.
ACTIVE.CELL	Returns the cell reference of the current cell.
CALLER	Returns the cell reference of the cell that started the function macro.
DEREF	Returns the value of a cell in a reference.
DOCUMENTS	Returns the name or names of an open document.
FILES	Returns the name or names of a file in a specified directory.
GET.BAR	Returns the number of the active menu bar.
GET.CELL	Returns information about a referenced cell.
GET.CHART.ITEM	Returns the location of a chart element in a chart.
GET.DEF	Returns a name matching a given definition.
GET.DOCUMENT	Returns information about a document.

GET.FORMULA	Returns the contents of a cell.
GET.NAME	Returns the definition of a name.
GET.NOTE	Returns the contents of a note.
GET.WINDOW	Returns information about a particular window.
GET.WORKSPACE	Returns information about the entire workspace.
LINKS	Returns the names of all linked files.
NAMES	Returns an array containing all of the defined names in a document.
OFFSET	Returns a reference offset from a given reference.
REFTEXT	Converts a reference into text.
RELREF	Returns a relative reference.
SELECTION	Returns the cell reference of a selection.
TEXTREF	Converts text to a reference.
WINDOWS	Returns the name or names of the open windows on your screen.

Appendix B
Quick Reference Guide *Excel* for the Apple Macintosh

Menus
Worksheet Menus

File Menu

New. . .
Open. . .
Links. . .
Close All
Save. . .
Save As. . .
Delete. . .
Page Setup. . .
Print. . .
Printer Setup. . .
Quit

Edit Menu

Undo
Cut
Copy
Paste
Clear. . .
Paste Special. . .
Delete. . .
Insert. . .

Fill Right
Fill Down

Formula Menu

Paste Name. . .
Paste Function. . .
Reference
Define Name. . .
Create Names. . .
Goto. . .
Find. . .
Select Last Cell
Show Active Cell

Format Menu

Number. . .
Alignment. . .
Style. . .
Border. . .
Cell Protection. . .
Column Width. . .

Data Menu

Find
Extract. . .
Delete
Set Database
Set Criteria
Sort. . .
Series. . .
Table. . .

Options Menu

Set Print Area
Set Print Titles
Set Page Break
Remove Page Break
Font
Display. . .

Freeze Panes
Protect Document. . .
Precision as Displayed
R1C1
Calculate Now
Calculation. . .

Macro Menu

Record. . .
Run. . .
Set Recorder
Start Recorder
Relative Record

Window Menu

Show Clipboard
New Window
Worksheet1

Help Menu (under About Excel on the Apple menu)

Context Sensitive Help
Canceling a Command
Saving Memory
Using a Network
Using Your Keyboard
File/Window Commands

Close All
Delete
New
New Window, Activate
Open, Links
Printing Commands
Save, Save As
Show Clipboard
Quit

The Worksheet Formula
Bar
Worksheet Commands

Alignment, Column Width

Calculate Now

Calculation

Cell/Document Protection

Cut, Copy, Clear

Define Name, Create
Names

Delete, Insert

Display

Fill Right, Fill Down

Freeze Panes

Font, Style, Border

Number

Paste, Paste Special

Paste Function

Paste Name

Precision as Displayed

Printing Commands

R1C1/A1

Reference

Selection Commands

Series

Table

Undo

Database Commands

Delete, Extract, Find

Set Criteria

Set Database

Sort

Macro Sheet Commands

Absolute/Relative Record

Define Name

Macro Language Functions

Run

Set Recorder

Start/Stop Recorder

Record. . .

Charting

Chart Commands

Add Arrow/Delete Arrow

Attach Text

Axes

Axis

Calculate Now

Clear, Cut

Copy

Copy Chart

Gallery Menu Commands

Legend

Main Chart

Overlay Chart

Paste, Paste Special

Patterns

Preferred, Set Preferred

Select Chart/Plot Area

Text

Undo

Chart Menus

File menu

New. . .

Open. . .

Links. . .

Close All

Save. . .

Save As. . .

Delete. . .

Page Setup. . .
Print. . .
Printer Setup. . .
Quit

Edit menu

Undo
Cut
Copy
Copy Chart. . .
Paste
Clear. . .
Paste Special. . .

Gallery menu

Area. . .
Bar. . .
Column. . .
Line. . .
Pie. . .
Scatter. . .
Combination. . .

Chart menu

Main Chart Type. . .
Overlay Chart Type. . .
Set Preferred Format
Axes. . .
Add Legend
Attach Text. . .
Add Arrow
Select Chart
Select Plot Area
Calculate Now

Format menu

Patterns. . .
Main Chart. . .
Overlay Chart. . .

Axis. . .

Legend. . .

Text. . .

Macro menu

Run. . .

Record. . .

Set Recorder

Start Recorder

Relative Record

Window menu

Show Clipboard

Chart1

Appendix C
Macro Functions

The list of macro commands and functions available with *Excel* for the IBM-AT and *Excel* for the Macintosh are slightly different, because of the revision dates for each product. As was mentioned at the beginning of the book, the IBM-AT version of *Excel* used for this book is version 2.0, while the Macintosh version of *Excel* is version 1.5.

Under most circumstances, this doesn't pose a problem. However, the difference shows up in the list of macro functions and commands available. The IBM version, being the later version, has more functions and commands than does the Macintosh version. When we talked with Microsoft, we were told that version 2.0 of *Excel* for the Macintosh will remove that disparity.

Macros

You can create two kinds of macros with *Excel:*

- Command macros carry out some sequence of actions, such as specifying commands, entering data, selecting cells, formatting, or selecting parts of a chart.
- Function macros operate like the worksheet functions, in that they use values for input, make calculations, and return the resulting values.

This appendix discusses both types of macros, grouped by how they work. Except for the command equivalent functions and dialog box functions, each category lists the macro commands and functions, along with appropriate arguments, and explains it. Many of the explanations contain examples showing how to use the command or function.

Command Equivalent Functions

When you execute a command equivalent function in a macro, you perform the same action as if you were choosing the equivalent command from a worksheet menu. Arguments specified with a command equivalent function specify options associated with the command.

Below, we show you the macro function that's equivalent to a worksheet command, and its comparable worksheet command.

The following macro functions work in both the IBM and Macintosh environments:

Macro Function	Worksheet Command Equivalent
ACTIVATE	Window (document)
ALIGNMENT	Format Alignment
BORDER	Format Border
CALCULATE.NOW	Chart Calculate Now
	Options Calculate Now
CALCULATION	Options Calculation
CANCEL.COPY	no equivalent; ends Copy
CELL.PROTECTION	Format Cell Protection
CHANGE.LINKS	File Links
CLEAR	Edit Clear
CLOSE	Control Close (document)
COLUMN.WIDTH	Format Column Width
COMBINATION	Gallery Combination
COPY	Edit Copy
COPY.CHART	Edit Copy Chart
COPY.PICTURE	Edit Copy Picture
CREATE.NAMES	Formula Create Names
CUT	Edit Cut
DATA.DELETE	Data Delete
DATA.FIND	Data Find
	Data Exit Find
DATA.SERIES	Data Series
DEFINE.NAME	Formula Define Name
DELETE.ARROW	Chart Delete Arrow
DELETE.NAME	Formula Define Name
DISPLAY	Info Cell
	Info Dependents

	Info Format
	Info Formula
	Info Names
	Info Note
	Info Precedents
	Info Protection
	Info Value
EDIT.DELETE	Edit Delete
EXTRACT	Data Extract
FILE.DELETE	File Delete
FILL.DOWN	Edit Fill Down
FILL.RIGHT	Edit Fill Right
FONT	Format Font
FORMAT.NUMBER	Format Number
FORMAT.SIZE	Format Size
FORMAT.TEXT	Format Text
FORMULA.FIND	Formula Find
FORMULA.GOTO	Formula Goto
FREEZE.PANES	Options Freeze Panes
FULL	Control Maximize (document)
	Control Restore (document)
GALLERY.AREA	Gallery Area
GALLERY.BAR	Gallery Bar
GALLERY.COLUMN	Gallery Column
GALLERY.LINE	Gallery Line
GALLERY.PIE	Gallery Pie
GALLERY.SCATTER	Gallery Scatter
INSERT	Edit Insert
LEGEND	Chart Add Legend
MAIN.CHART	Format Main Chart
MOVE	Control Move (document)
NEW	File New
NEW.WINDOW	Window New Window
OPEN	File Open
OPEN.LINKS	File Links

OVERLAY.CHART.TYPE	Chart Overlay Chart Type
PAGE.SETUP	File Page Setup
PASTE	Edit Paste
PASTE.SPECIAL	Edit Paste Special
PRECISION	Options Calculation
PREFERRED	Gallery Preferred
PRINT	File Print
PRINTER.SETUP	File Printer Setup
PROTECT.DOCUMENT	Chart Protect Document
	Chart Unprotect Document
	Options Protect Document
QUIT	File Exit
	Control Close (application)
REMOVE.PAGE.BREAK	Options Remove Page Break
RUN	Macro run
SAVE	File Save
SAVE.AS	File Save As
SELECT.CHART	Chart Select Chart
	Chart Select Plot Area
SELECT.SPECIAL	Formula Select Special
SELECT.LAST.CELL	Formula Select Last Cell
SET.CRITERIA	Data Set Criteria
SET.DATABASE	Data Set Database
SET.PAGE.BREAK	Options Set Page Break
SET.PREFERRED	Gallery Set Preferred
SET.PRINT.AREA	Options Set Print Area
SET.PRINT.TITLES	Options Set Print Titles
SHOW.ACTIVE.CELL	Formula Show Active Cell
SHOW.CLIPBOARD	Window Show Clipboard
SIZE	Control Size (document)
SORT	Data Sort
SPLIT	Control Split
TABLE	Data Table
UNDO	Edit Undo

The following macro functions work only in the IBM environment:

Macro Function	Worksheet Command Equivalent
ADD.ARROW	Chart Add Arrow
ADD.OVERLAY	Chart Add Overlay
APP.MAXIMIZE	Control Maximize (application)
APP.MINIMIZE	Control Minimize (application)
APP.MOVE	Control Move (application)
APP.RESTORE	Control Restore (application)
APP.SIZE	Control Size (application)
APPLY.NAMES	Formula Apply Names
ARRANGE.ALL	Window Arrange All
ATTACH.TEXT	Chart Attach Text
AXES	Chart Axes
CALCULATE.DOCUMENT	Chart Calculate Document
	Options Calculate Document
CLOSE.ALL	File Close All
DATA.FORM	Data Form
DELETE.OVERLAY	Chart Delete Overlay
FILE.CLOSE	File Close
FILL.LEFT	Edit Fill Left
FILL.UP	Edit Fill Up
FORMAT.FONT	Format Font
FORMAT.LEGEND	Format Legend
FORMAT.MOVE	Format Move
FORMULA.REPLACE	Formula Replace
GRIDLINES	Chart Gridlines
HIDE	Window Hide
JUSTIFY	Format Justify
LIST.NAMES	Formula Paste Name
NOTE	Formula Note
OVERLAY	Format Overlay
PARSE	Data Parse
PATTERNS	Format Patterns
PASTE.LINK	Edit Paste Link

REPLACE.FONT	Format Font
ROW.HEIGHT	Format Row Height
SAVE.WORKSPACE	File Save Workspace
SCALE	Format Scale
SHORT.MENUS	Options Full Menus
	Options Short Menus
	Chart Full Menus
	Chart Short Menus
SHOW.INFO	Window Show Document
	Window Show Info
UNHIDE	File Unhide Window
	Window Unhide
WORKSPACE	Options Workspace

Dialog Box Functions

Dialog box functions are available for every command that brings up a dialog box. Each dialog box function has the same name as the command equivalent function. The only difference is that the function is stated with a question mark.

For instance, the dialog box function for File Save As is SAVE.AS? The dialog box function for Edit Insert is INSERT?

Some dialog box functions don't display dialog boxes. We'll look at these individually in the sections below.

Note: the dialog box functions we mention here are not the same as the macro functions you use to create custom dialog boxes. Those are discussed separately, under *Customizing Functions*.

Action Equivalent Functions

The action equivalent functions listed below neither have command equivalents nor are they dialog box functions. Arguments are shown in parentheses. Remember that, if parentheses are shown, they must be included in the function as used, even if they include no arguments.

A1.R1C1(*r1c1*)

Displays A1 or R1C1 references

Works the same as choosing the Options Workspace command and turning on the R1C1 check box if the *r1c1* argument is true, or turning off the R1C1 check box if the *r1c1* argument is false.

ACTIVATE(*windowtext,panenumber*)
Selects a window

Works the same as activating a pane in a window. *Windowtext* is the name of a window and must be enclosed in double quote marks; *panenumber* is the number of the pane to activate.

ACTIVATE.NEXT( )
Selects the next window

Equivalent to pressing Ctrl-F6.

ACTIVATE.PREV( )
Selects the previous window

Equivalent to pressing Ctrl-Shift-F6.

CANCEL.COPY( )
Cancels the selected cell for a copy operation

Equivalent to canceling the box around a selected cell, by pressing the Esc key after you copy or cut a selection.

COPY.CHART(*number*)
Copies a picture of a chart

The picture shown depends on the number indicated:

Number	Picture Shown
1	As shown on the screen
2	As shown when printed

The COPY.CHART?(*number*) is acceptable in the Macintosh version. In *Microsoft Excel* for *Windows,* this is the same as the COPY.PICTURE macro function without the *appearance* argument.

DATA.FIND.NEXT( )
Finds the next matching record in a database

DATA.FIND.PREV( )
Finds the previous matching record in a database

Finds the next or the previous matching record in a database. If no matching record can be found, the function returns the value FALSE.

In the IBM environment, these functions work the same as pressing the up- or down-arrow keys after choosing the Data Find command, respectively. In the Macintosh environment, these functions work the same as pressing Command-F or Command–Shift-F, respectively.

DELETE.FORMAT(*formattext*)
Deletes a Format Number command format

Works the same as using the Format Number command to delete the format specified, where *formattext* is the format string and enclosed in double quotes, for instance, "#,##0".

DIRECTORY(*pathtext*)
Changes directories and returns a new path name

Sets the current drive and directory to the path given in *pathtext,* and returns the name of the new path as text. If a drive or directory name is not included in *pathtext,* it assumes the current drive or directory and returns that name.

FORMULA(*formulatext,reference*)
Enters a formula in a cell, or text on a chart

This function works differently, depending on whether the active document is a worksheet or a chart.

If the active document is a worksheet, the function enters the formula specified by *formulatext* into the cell specified by *reference.* If no cell is specified, it uses the active cell.

The formula must be in the form it would be if you entered it in the formula bar, but must be enclosed in double quotation marks. It can be a formula, a number, text, or a logical value. However, any cell references in a formula must be in R1C1 form. (If you're using the Recorder, *Excel* converts any A1-style references to R1C1 style.)

In the IBM environment, if the active document is a chart, *Excel* enters text labels or SERIES functions. If *formulatext* can be treated as a text label, and the current selection is a text label, the selected text label is replaced with *formulatext*. If the current selection is not a text label, the function creates a new text label. If *formulatext* can be treated as a SERIES formula, and the current selection is a SERIES formula, *formulatext* replaces the selected SERIES formula. If the current selection is not a SERIES formula, the function creates a new SERIES formula.

Examples

= FORMULA(625)

Enters the value 625 in the active cell

= FORMULA(" = R6C[− 1]*(1 + R8C10)")

Enters the formula = F6*(1 + $J$8) into the active cell if the active cell is G6

= FORMULA(" = SERIES(" "Name" ",,{1,2,3},1")

Enters a SERIES formula on the chart. Note that, within the text value, you have to enter two sets of double quotation marks in order to represent a single quotation mark.

FORMULA.ARRAY(*formulatext,reference*)
Enters an array formula on a document

Works the same as entering an array formula while pressing Ctrl-Shift-Enter in the IBM environment, or Command-Enter in the Macintosh environment. The function enters the formula specified in *formulatext* as an array formula in the range specified by *reference*, or in the current selection if *reference* is not given.

FORMULA.FILL(*formulatext,reference*)
Fills a range with a formula

Works the same as entering a formula while pressing Shift in the IBM environment, or Option in the Macintosh environment. The function enters the formula specified in *formulatext* into the area specified in *reference*, or in the current selection if reference is not given.

FORMULA.FIND.NEXT( )
Finds the next cell, as described in the Formula Find dialog box

FORMULA.FIND.PREV( )
Finds the previous cell, as described in the Formula Find dialog box

These two functions work the same as pressing F7, and Shift-F7, respectively, in the IBM environment, or Command-H or Command-Shift-H in the Macintosh environment, respectively.

The function finds the next or previous matching cells on the worksheet, as defined in the Formula Find dialog box. If no match is found, the function returns the value FALSE.

HLINE(*numbercols*)
Horizontally scrolls the active window by columns

This function scrolls the worksheet a number of columns to the right or left, depending on the number given in *numbercols*. If the number is positive, the worksheet scrolls to the right that number of columns; if the number is negative, the worksheet scrolls to the left that number of columns.

HPAGE(*numberwindows*)
Horizontally scrolls the active window one full window at a time

This function scrolls the worksheet a number of windows to the right or left, depending on the number given in *numberwindows*. If the number is positive, the worksheet scrolls to the right that number of windows; if the number is negative, the worksheet scrolls to the left that number of windows.

195

HSCROLL(*scroll,value*)

Horizontally scrolls a document by percentage or by column number

HSCROLL lets you scroll to the right or left edge of your document, or anywhere in between. If *value* is TRUE, HSCROLL scrolls to the position represented by the number you specify as *scroll*. If *value* is FALSE or omitted, HSCROLL scrolls to the position represented by the fraction given in *scroll*. If *scroll* is 0, HSCROLL scrolls to the left edge of your document; if *scroll* is 1, it scrolls to the right edge of your document.

To scroll to a specific column, either use the form HSCROLL(*colnumber*,TRUE) or HSCROLL(*colnumber*/256).

Examples

Assuming you're starting from A1, the following uses of HSCROLL all scroll to column 64—which is 25 percent of the way across the worksheet:

HSCROLL(64,TRUE)
HSCROLL(25%)
HSCROLL(.25,FALSE)
HSCROLL(64/256)

SELECT(*selection,activecell*)

Selects a reference

This is one of two forms of the SELECT function. This is the one used if the selection is on a worksheet or macro sheet. (The following version is used if the selection refers to a chart.)

This function is used to select a cell or cell range, as specified in *selection*, and to make *activecell* the active cell. Both arguments must be preceded with exclamation marks if the A1 reference style is used.

Selection must be either a reference on the active worksheet (for instance, !B23:C24, !Netsales, or an R1C1-style reference to the currently active cell such as "R[−1]C5:"). If you omit selection, SELECT does not change the selection.

Activecell must be within *selection*, and may be either a reference to a single cell on the active worksheet, such as !B23, or an

R1C1-style reference to the active cell in the current selection, as was shown in the preceding paragraph.

If you're recording a macro with the Macro Relative Record command and you select something, *Excel* uses R1C1-style references as text. If you're using Macro Absolute Record, *Excel* uses absolute references.

SELECT(*itemtext*)

(For PC Only) Selects an item on a chart

This is one of two forms of the SELECT function. This is the one used if the selection is a chart. The preceding version is used if the selection refers to a worksheet or macro sheet.

Itemtext must be enclosed in double quotation marks, and refers to a chart object, as follows:

Itemtext	Selection
''Chart''	Entire chart
''Plot''	Plot area
''Legend''	Legend
''Axis 1''	Main chart value axis
''Axis 2''	Main chart category axis
''Axis 3''	Overlay chart value axis
''Axis 4''	Overlay chart category axis
''Title''	Chart title
''Text Axis 1''	Label for main chart value axis
''Text Axis 2''	Label for main chart category axis
''Text n''	nth floating text item
''Arrow n''	nth arrow
''Gridline 1''	Major gridlines of value axis
''Gridline 2''	Minor gridlines of value axis
''Gridline 3''	Major gridlines of category axis
''Gridline 4''	Minor gridlines of category axis
''Dropline 1''	Main chart droplines
''Dropline 2''	Overlay chart droplines
''Hiloline 1''	Main chart hi-lo lines
''Hiloline 2''	Overlay chart hi-lo lines

"S*n*P*x*"	Data associated with point *x* in series *n*
"Text S*n*P*x*"	Text attached to point *x* of series *n*
"Text S*n*"	Series title text of series *n* of an area chart

SELECT.END(direction#)

(For PC Only) Changes the active cell

Moves the active cell to the edge of the next block, in the direction specified by *direction#*:

Direction#	Direction
1	Left (same as Ctrl-left arrow)
2	Right (same as Ctrl-right arrow)
3	Up (same as Ctrl-up arrow)
4	Down (same as Ctrl-down arrow)

SELECT.LAST.CELL( )

Selects the cell at the end of a document

Selects the cell at the intersection of the last row and last column in your document that contains a formula, value, or format, or is referred to in a formula.

SHOW.ACTIVE.CELL( )

Displays the active cell

Scrolls the active window so the active cell becomes visible. Works the same as pressing Ctrl-Backspace in the IBM environment, or choosing the Formula Show Active Cell command in the Macintosh environment.

SHOW.CLIPBOARD( )

Displays the Clipboard

Works the same as choosing the Run command on the Control menu, and selecting Clipboard in the IBM environment, or choosing the Window Show Clipboard environment in the Macintosh environment.

STYLE(*bold,italic*)

STYLE?(*bold,italic*)
Changes font

If *bold* is TRUE, *Excel* finds an available bold font and changes the font of the current selection to the bold font. If *italic* is TRUE, it changes the font of the current selection to an available italic font. If no appropriate font is available, *Excel* uses the most similar font available.

In the Macintosh environment, this is equivalent to choosing the Format Style command.

UNLOCKED.NEXT( )
Moves to the next unlocked cell

UNLOCKED.PREV( )
Moves to the previous unlocked cell

Works the same as pressing Tab or Shift-Tab, respectively, in the IBM environment, or Enter or Shift-Enter, respectively, in the Macintosh environment, to move the active cell to the next or previous unlocked cell in a protected worksheet.

VLINE(*numberrows*)
Vertically scrolls the active window by rows

Scrolls the active window vertically the number of rows specified in *numberrows*. If *numberrows* is positive, *Excel* scrolls down; if *numberrows* is negative, *Excel* scrolls up.

VPAGE(*numberwindows*)
Vertically scrolls the active window one window at a time

Scrolls the active window vertically the number of windows specified in *numberwindows*. If *numberwindows* is positive, *Excel* scrolls down. If *numberwindows* is negative, *Excel* scrolls up.

VSCROLL(*scroll, value*)

Vertically scrolls the document by percentage or by row number

VSCROLL lets you scroll to the top or bottom of your window, or anywhere in between. If *value* is TRUE, VSCROLL scrolls to the row represented by the number you specify as *scroll*. If *value* is FALSE or omitted, VSCROLL scrolls to the position represented by the fraction given in *scroll*. If *scroll* is 0, VSCROLL scrolls to the top row, row 1; if *scroll* is 1, it scrolls to the bottom of the window, row 16384.

To scroll to a specific row, either use the form VSCROLL(*rownumber,*TRUE) or VSCROLL(*rownumber*/16384).

Examples

Assuming you're starting from A1, the following uses of VSCROLL all scroll to row 4096—or 25 percent of the way down the window:

HSCROLL(4096,TRUE)
HSCROLL(25%)
HSCROLL(.25,FALSE)
HSCROLL(4096/16384)

Customizing Functions
ADD.BAR( )

Adds a custom menu bar

Creates an empty menu bar, and if successful, returns the bar ID number. If 15 menu bars (the maximum number of custom menu bars allowed) have already been defined, ADD.BAR returns the error message #VALUE!.

ADD.BAR doesn't display the new bar. To see the bar, use the SHOW.BAR function.

ADD.COMMAND(*bar#,menuposition,menureference*)

Adds a custom command

Adds one or more custom commands described in the menu construction area *menureference* to the menu, at *menuposition* in bar number *bar#*. *Menureference* must be to a macro sheet that describes the new command.

Menuposition can be the number of a menu or the text name of a menu. *Bar#* can be the number of one of the built-in menu bars or the ID number returned by the previously executed ADD.BAR function. The command position of the first command added is returned by the ADD.COMMAND.

Built-in menu bar numbers are:

Number	Built-in Menu Bar
1	Worksheet and macro menu, full menus
2	Chart menu, full menus
3	Nil menu (menu displayed when no documents are open)

The following additional numbers are valid only in the IBM environment:

Number	Built-in Menu Bar
4	Info window menu
5	Worksheet and macro menu, short menus
6	Chart menu, short menus

ADD.MENU(*bar#,menureference*)
Adds a custom menu

Adds a menu described in the menu construction area *menureference* to the bar with the bar ID number *bar#*. *Menureference* must be to a macro sheet that describes the new menu.

Bar# can be the number of one of the built-in menu bars or the ID number returned by the previously executed ADD.BAR function.

If ADD.MENU is successful, the menu is added immediately to the right of the existing menus on bar *bar#*, and ADD.MENU returns the position number of the new menu.

ALERT(*messagetext,type#*)
Displays a dialog box

This is the function to use if you want to display a custom dialog box and have the user choose a button.

The dialog box contains the text you specify as *messagetext*,

and the type of box display depends on the number you specify
as *type#*:

Type#	Used For
1	Telling the user to make a choice (see Figure B-1)
2	Presenting info (see Figure B-2)
3	Error message where no choice is available (see Figure B-3)

Figure B-1. Choice Dialog Box

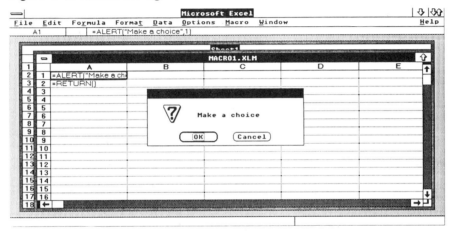

Figure B-2. Information Dialog Box

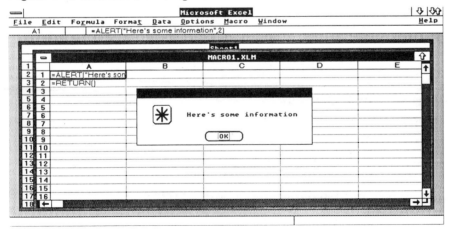

Figure B-3. Error Message Dialog Box

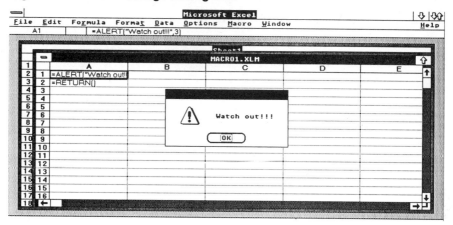

ALERT returns the logical value TRUE if the user chooses the OK bar, and FALSE if the Cancel bar is chosen.

Examples

ALERT("I'm sorry, Dave, I'm afraid I can't do that.",3)

Figure B-4. Alert Dialog Box

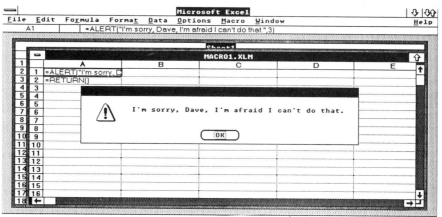

ALERT("Data entered will affect other worksheets.",1)

Figure B-5. Alert Dialog Box

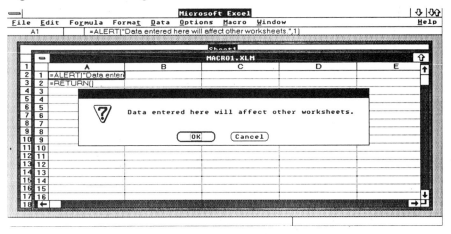

APP.ACTIVATE(*titletext,waitvalue*)

(For PC Only) Starts another application

Use this function to activate another application with the title bar *titletext*. If *titletext* is omitted, the function activates *Excel*.

The argument *waitvalue* is used to tell *Excel* to wait before starting the application. If *waitvalue* is TRUE or is omitted, *Excel* flashes a message indicating it is waiting. If *waitvalue* is FALSE, *Excel* activates the application immediately.

BEEP(*number*)

BEEP( )

Sounds a warning beep

BEEP triggers production of an audible tone.

BEEP(*number*) is the form used in the IBM environment. Depending on your hardware, you may be able to use the argument number to specify different tones. Number may be from 1 to 4, and is interpreted by your hardware as a beep tone. Some hardware (for example an IBM-PC) interpret all numbers used with BEEP as the same tone.

BEEP( ) is the form used in the Macintosh environment. You control the volume with the Control Panel desk accessory.

CALL(*calltext, argument1,. . .*)

(For IBM Only) Calls the *Microsoft Windows* library

204

CALL is suggested for use only by programmers expert in using the *Microsoft Windows* dynamic library. Incorrect use could cause damage to your system's operation.

CALL works with the macro function REGISTER, which sets up the parameters for CALL. In using REGISTER, you specify the name of the module and procedure you want to use, as well as a text value describing the number and data types of arguments you want to give, and the data type of the return value. REGISTER returns the value of *calltext* to use with the CALL function.

CANCEL.KEY(*enable,macroreference*)

(For IBM Only) Alters the Esc key

Lets you temporarily disable the Esc key during a currently running macro. If *enable* is FALSE or omitted, pressing Esc while a macro is running will not interrupt it. If *enable* is TRUE and *macroreference* is omitted, the Esc key is reactivated. If enable is TRUE and you specify *macroreference*, execution jumps to the specified macro location if you press Esc.

CANCEL.KEY only lasts for the duration of the currently running macro. Once the macro stops, the Esc key is reactivated.

CHECK.COMMAND(*bar#,menuposition,commandposition,check*)

Marks a command

Adds or removes a check mark beside the command designated. *Bar#* is either the number of one of the *Excel* built-in menu bars, or the number returned by the previously executed ADD.BAR function. (In the Macintosh environment, the Apple desk accessory menu is not numbered and can't be referred to.) *Menuposition* is either the number of the menu or the text form of the menu name. *Commandposition* is either the number of the command or the text form of the command title.

If *check* is TRUE, this function checks the command; if *check* is FALSE, it removes the check mark.

A check mark does not affect the execution of the command. Its primary use is to indicate a command or option is in effect.

DELETE.BAR(*bar#*)

Deletes a custom menu bar

Deletes the custom menu bar numbered *bar#*. *Bar#* must be the number returned by the previously ADD.BAR function, and may not be the currently displayed menu bar.

DELETE.COMMAND(*bar#*,*menuposition*,*commandposition*)

Deletes a command

Deletes the command in the position specified. *Bar#* is either the number of one of the *Excel* built-in menu bars, or the number returned by the previously executed ADD.BAR function. *Menuposition* is either the number of the menu or the text form of the menu name.

Commandposition is either the number of the command or the text form of the command title.

If the specified command doesn't exist, the function returns the error message #VALUE!

When a command is deleted, the number used for *commandposition* for all commands after that is decreased by 1.

DELETE.MENU(*bar#*,*menuposition*)

Deletes a menu

Deletes the menu at *menuposition* in the bar identified by *bar#*. *Menuposition* is either the number of the menu or the text form of the menu name. *Bar#* is either the number of one of the *Excel* built-in menu bars, or the number returned by the previously executed ADD.BAR function.

If the menu specified by *menuposition* does not exist, the function returns the error message #VALUE!.

When a menu has been deleted, the number used for menuposition for all menus to the right of that menu is decreased by 1.

DIALOG.BOX(*dialogreference*)

Displays a custom dialog box

Displays the dialog box described in the construction area described in *dialogreference*, which may be on a macro sheet or a worksheet. The area pointed to by *dialogreference* must be seven columns wide and at least two rows high.

If the OK bar in the dialog box is chosen, the function enters values in the fields as specified in the *dialogreference* area, and returns the item number of the button pressed. Items are numbered sequentially, starting with the item in the second row in *dialogreference*. If the Cancel button in the dialog box is chosen, the function returns FALSE.

If *dialogreference* is invalid, the function returns the error message #VALUE!, and when the macro is run, displays a message indicating the cell in which the error was found.

DISABLE.INPUT(*logicalvalue*)
(For IBM Only) Stops all input to *Excel*

If *logicalvalue* is TRUE, the function blocks all input from the keyboard and mouse, except input to display in dialog boxes. If *logicalvalue* is FALSE, input is reenabled.

ECHO(*logicalvalue*)
Toggles screen update on and off

If *logicalvalue* is TRUE or omitted, the function turns on screen updating while a macro is running. If *logicalvalue* is FALSE, it turns off the screen updating. Screen updating resumes automatically when a macro ends.

ECHO is particularly useful when running a large command macro, since turning off screen updating lets the macro run faster.

ENABLE.COMMAND(*bar#,menuposition,commandposition,enable*)
Toggles the graying of a custom command

Enables or disables the command identified by the arguments. *Bar#* is either the number of one of the *Excel* built-in menu bars, or the number returned by the previously executed ADD.BAR function. *Menuposition* is either the number of the menu or the text form of the menu name. *Commandposition* is either the number of the command to be checked or the text form of the command title. If *commandposition* is 0, the entire menu is enabled or disabled.

If *enable* is TRUE, the function enables the command. If *enable* is FALSE, the function disables the command. Disabled commands appear grayed and cannot be executed.

If the specified command is one of *Excel's* built-in commands, or doesn't exist, the function returns the error message #VALUE!

ERROR(*enable,macroreference*)

Specifies an action to take if an error occurs while a macro is running

If *enable* is FALSE, all error checking is disabled. When error checking of a macro has been disabled, and an error is encountered, *Excel* ignores it and continues.

If *enable* is TRUE, and *macroreference* is omitted, normal error checking occurs, which means a dialog box appears when an error is encountered, permitting you to halt execution, single-step through the macro, or continue normal running. If *enable* is TRUE and *macroreference* specifies the reference of a macro, that macro will be run when an error is encountered.

Warning: Both ERROR(TRUE,*macroreference*) and ERROR(FALSE) result in no warning messages at all. ERROR(FALSE) further suppresses the warning messages that normally are displayed if you attempt to close an unsaved document.

EXEC(*programtext,window#*)

(For IBM Only) Starts another application

Starts the program named *programtext* as a separate program running under *Microsoft Windows* version 2.0. *Programtext* uses the same form of arguments as the File Run command in the *Windows* MS-DOS Executive.

Window# specifies how the window holding the program should appear:

Window#	Window Type
1	Normal window
2	Minimized window
3	Maximized window

If omitted, *window#* is assumed to be 2.

If the EXEC function is successful, it returns the task ID number of the program started. The task ID number identifies the program running under *Microsoft Windows* version 2.0 or higher. If

the function is unsuccessful, it returns the error message
#VALUE!

EXECUTE(*channel#*,*executetext*)

(For IBM Only) Carries out a command in another application

The EXECUTE function executes whatever commands are described in *executetext* in the application that's connected through *channel#*. The channel so designated must have already been opened by the INITIATE macro function.

This function works only if you are running *Microsoft Windows* version 2.0 or higher.

EXECUTE returns the following error messages if unsuccessful:

Message	Meaning
#VALUE!	*Channel#* isn't a valid channel number.
#N/A!	The application is doing something else.
#DIV/0!	The application doesn't respond, so you've pressed Esc to cancel the command.
#REF!	The application refuses the EXECUTE request.

FCLOSE(*file#*)

(For IBM Only) Closes a text file

Closes the file that has been opened with FOPEN (following). *File#* is the number of the file, and has been returned when FOPEN completed successfully.

FOPEN(*filetext*,*access#*)

(For IBM Only) Opens a text file

FOPEN opens the file named *filetext*, and returns a file number. The argument *access#* specifies the type of access to allow to the file:

Access#	Type of Access
1	Read/write access
2	Read-only access
3	Create new file, with read/write access

209

If the file doesn't exist and *access#* is 3, FOPEN creates a new file. If it doesn't exist and *access#* is 1 or 2, or if FOPEN can't open the file, FOPEN returns the error message #N/A!

FPOS(*file#*,*position#*)
(For IBM Only) Returns position in a text file

Once a file has been opened with FOPEN and *file#* returned, the FPOS function looks in the file so identified and positions the file (for further activity, such as reading or writing) at *position#* within the file. (The first byte of the file is considered position 1.)

FREAD(*file#*,*#characters*)
(For IBM Only) Reads characters from a text file

Reads *#characters* from the file *file#*, where *file#* is the number returned when FOPEN was used to open the file.

If FREAD is successful, it returns the text read. If *file#* isn't a valid file number, it returns the error message #VALUE!. If FREAD can't read the document, or if it reaches the end of the file, it returns the error message #N/A!

FREADLN(*file#*)
(For IBM Only) Reads a line from a text file

FREADLN starts at the current file position (see FPOS) in the file identified by *file#* and reads till it encounters an End of Line character or equivalent. The file must have been opened with FOPEN, and *file#* is the number returned by that function.

FSIZE(*file#*)
(For IBM Only) Returns the size of a text file

Returns the number of characters in the file identified by *file#*, which is the number returned by the function FOPEN.

If file# is not a valid file number, FSIZE returns the error message #VALUE!

FWRITE(*file#*,*text*)
(For IBM Only) Writes characters to a text file

FWRITE writes the characters in text to the file identified by *file#*, starting at the current position (see FPOS). The file must have been opened by FOPEN, which returns *file#*.

If *file#* is not a valid file number, FWRITE returns the error message #VALUE!. If it can't write to the file, it returns the error message #N/A!

FWRITELN(*file#*, *text*)

(For IBM Only) Writes line to a text file

FWRITELN writes the characters specified in text to the file identified by *file#*, starting at the current position in that file (see FPOS). The characters written are followed by the character pair carriage return and line feed.

The file must have been opened by FOPEN, which returns *file#*.

If *file#* is not a valid file number, FWRITELN returns the error message #VALUE!. If it can't write to the file, it returns the error message #N/A!

HELP(*helptext*)

(For IBM Only) Displays a customized Help topic

When used as a macro function, HELP displays the Help topic specified as *helptext*, where *helptext* is a reference to a topic in a custom help file in the form *filename!topic#*. If you omit *helptext*, HELP displays the normal *Excel* Help index.

INITIATE(*applicationtext, topictext*)

(For IBM Only) Opens a channel to another application

INITIATE opens a DDE channel to another application, but doesn't start the application. *Applicationtext* is the DDE name of the application you want. *Topictext* describes what you want to access. This can be a filename, or whatever is appropriate for the application.

If INITIATE is successful, it returns the number of the open channel, and all subsequent DDE macro functions will use this number when specifying a channel.

When an application is running, it will have a task number; if more than one instance of the application is running, this task

number is necessary to identify which instance you want. If you
don't specify a task number and more than one instance is running, INITIATE displays a dialog box, allowing you to identify
the instance you want.

INPUT(*prompt, type, title, default, xposition, yposition*)

INPUT(*prompt, type, title*)
Displays a dialog box

INPUT displays a dialog box, and returns the information in
the dialog box. The form with six arguments is used in the IBM
environment; the form with three arguments is used in the Macintosh environment.

Prompt and *type* are required arguments, and are text. *Title*,
default, *xposition*, and *yposition* are optional; *title* is text and the
other three arguments must be numbers.

INPUT is one way you can design a custom dialog box, and
is particularly useful for prompting the user to enter data.

An INPUT dialog box looks like this:

Figure B-6. INPUT Dialog Box

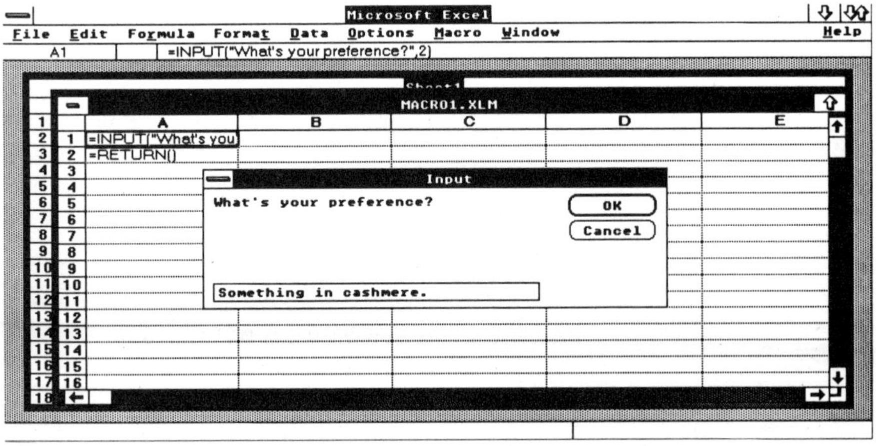

If you omit *title*, *Excel* assumes it's *Input*. If you omit *xposition*
or *yposition*, *Excel* assumes they are 0 and centers the dialog box.

The argument *type* refers to the data type that's expected to be entered:

Number	Data Type
0	Formula
1	Number
2	Text
4	Logical
8	Reference
16	Error
64	Array

Excel allows you to indicate a combination of types, by summing the numeric values. For instance, if you want the input box to accept numbers, text, or logical values, but not cell references, set *type* = 7.

When you set *type* = 8, INPUT returns the absolute cell reference. When you set *type* = 0, INPUT returns the formula as text, with any references set in R1C1 style.

If the information entered by the user isn't the correct type, *Excel* tries to translate it to the correct type. If it can't, it displays an error message.

MESSAGE(*logical, text*)

Displays a message in status bar

Toggles the display or removal of a message (*text*) in the status bar. Any message displayed with MESSAGE stays in the status bar until removed by another MESSAGE.

If *logical* is TRUE, *Excel* displays text in the status bar. If *text* is the empty text value (" "), any message currently displayed in the status bar is removed. If *logical* is FALSE, any message in the status bar is removed and the status bar is reenabled to handle normal command help messages.

ON.DATA(*documenttext, macrotext*)

(For IBM Only) Runs a macro when data is sent to *Excel* by another application

ON.DATA lets you automatically update a document whenever it receives new data. *Macrotext* is the name of the macro that's started when new data is sent by another application to the document specified by *documenttext*. *Macrotext* must be a text form of R1C1-style reference.

If the incoming data causes recalculation, *Excel* first does the recalculating, then starts the macro specified.

ON.DATA stays in effect until either you turn it off or you quit *Excel*. If you close the macro sheet containing *macrotext*, an error message is generated when data is sent to the document named in *documenttext*. To turn off ON.DATA, omit the *macrotext* argument.

ON.KEY(*keytext,macrotext*)

(For IBM Only) Runs a macro when a particular key is pressed

ON.KEY lets you set up an autokey initiation of your macro. When you press the key specified in *keytext*, the macro specified in *macrotext* is run.

The key specified in *keytext* must be in a form *Excel* can understand. The Appendix on pages 373–375 of the *Microsoft Excel Functions and Macros* manual explains how to specify keys.

Macrotext must be a text form of R1C1-style reference. If *macrotext* is empty text (" "), nothing happens when the key is pressed. If *macrotext* is omitted, *keytext* reverts to its normal meaning.

ON.KEY remains in effect until you turn it off or you quit *Excel*.

ON.TIME(*time,macrotext,tolerance,insertvalue*)

(For IBM Only) Runs a macro at a certain time

ON.TIME lets you set up your worksheet so a macro is run at a specific time. It uses the time portion of the serial number that is automatically updated to current date and time when you turn on your machine.

Macrotext is the R1C1-style reference to the macro that is to be run. If *insertvalue* is TRUE or is omitted, the macro will be run at the *time* specified. If *insertvalue* is FALSE, any prior requests to execute the specified macro at the specified *time* are ignored.

The *time* argument can be a number less than 1; if so, *Excel* will assume that the macro is to be run every day at the time specified. If the specified time occurs and the macro specified is not in memory, the function is ignored. If two identical ON.TIME statements are present, the first is executed, and the second is ignored and returns the error message #N/A!

The *tolerance* parameter is used to allow *Excel* to leave one of the modes where this function can be executed, then return and still run the function. If the specified time occurs and *Excel* is not in READY, COPY, CUT, or FIND mode, *Excel* waits for the length of time specified by *tolerance* (a date/time serial number). If *Excel* doesn't return to one of these modes within the length of time specified, the request is canceled.

ON.WINDOW(*windowtext,macrotext*)

(For IBM Only) Runs a macro when a window is changed

ON.WINDOW starts the macro specified in *macrotext* whenever the window specified in *windowtext* is activated. Both arguments must be enclosed in double quotes.

If *windowtext* is omitted, *Excel* starts the macro specified whenever any window is activated, except for those windows named in other ON.WINDOW functions.

POKE(*channel#,itemtext,datareference*)

(For IBM Only) Sends data to another application

POKE lets you send data from *Excel* to another application while both *Excel* and the other application are running.

POKE uses the channel number returned by the INITIATE function. *Itemtext* is the specification within the other application where the data is to go, and *datareference* is the reference to the cell or cell range where the *Excel* data is to be found.

If POKE is not successful because the channel number isn't valid, it returns the error message #VALUE!. If POKE is refused, it returns the error message #REF!. If the application you're trying to send data to does not respond and you press the Esc key to cancel the request, POKE returns the error message #DIV/0!

REGISTER(*moduletext,proceduretext,argumenttext*)

(For IBM Only) Accesses *Microsoft Windows* library

This is a very powerful function that returns a text value to be used by the CALL function, which in turn can then be used to access the *Microsoft Windows* dynamic library.

Basically a system-level command, REGISTER must be used with considerable care, or it could cause system operation errors.

The argument *moduletext* contains the name of the *Microsoft Windows* dynamic library that contains the procedure you want. *Proceduretext* is the text form of the procedure name you want. *Argumenttext* is a character string with argument codes concatenated with return type codes.

REGISTER is a complex function, requiring system-level understanding of the *Microsoft Windows* dynamic library. It's discussed in more detail in the companion book, *PC Excel Business Solutions*.

RENAME.COMMAND
(*bar#,menuposition,commandposition,nametext*)
Renames command

Assigns the name specified in *nametext* to a command at a specified position on a specified menu. *Menuposition* can either be the number of a menu or its name as text. *Commandposition* can either be the number of the command being renamed or its title as text. If *commandposition* is 0, the menu is renamed.

Bar# is either the number of the built-in menu bars or the number returned by the previously executed ADD.BAR function.

If the command specified does not exist, the function returns the error message #VALUE!

REQUEST(*channel#,itemtext*)
(For IBM Only) Returns data from another application

REQUEST gets the data specified by *itemtext* from the application connected via *channel#*. *Channel#* is the number of a channel that has already been opened by INITIATE. REQUEST returns data as an array.

If the channel number specified is not valid, REQUEST returns the error message #VALUE!. If the request is refused, it returns the error message #REF!. If the application is busy, the function returns the error value #N/A!. If the application doesn't respond and you press the Esc key to cancel the function, it returns the error message #DIV/0!

SEND.KEYS(*keytext,waitvalue*)

(For IBM Only) Sends a key sequence to an application

SEND.KEYS lets you send a keystroke sequence to another application, just as if you had pressed the keys in that application. The keys should be in the form described in the Appendix, pages 373–375, of the *Excel Functions and Macros Reference* manual.

If *waitvalue* is TRUE, *Excel* waits for the keys to be processed before returning control to the calling macro. If *waitvalue* is FALSE or omitted, the macro continues without waiting for the other application to process the keys.

SET.NAME(*nametext,value*)

Defines a name as a certain value

SET.NAME is the same as equating a named variable with a constant, a logical value, or a reference. If *value* is omitted, the name *nametext* is deleted.

If you use SET.NAME to define *nametext* as a reference, it will be the text version of that reference, not the value. If you want the value of that reference, use the DEREF function.

SET.VALUE(*reference,values*)

Enters values in a cell

SET.VALUE changes the value of the cell or cells specified in reference to the values specified, unless a cell already contains a formula, in which case it's ignored.

The cells referred to by reference must be cells on the current macro sheet. If reference is a range, values should be an equivalent size array of numbers. If there's a mismatch, *Excel* expands the array to fit the range.

SHOW.BAR(*bar#*)

Displays a menu bar

SHOW.BAR displays the menu bar specified by *bar#*, where *bar#* can be either one of the built-in menu bars, or the number returned by the previously executed ADD.BAR. If *bar#* is omitted, *Excel* displays a standard bar, depending on which window is active:

If Active Window Has	Standard bar
Worksheet or macro sheet (full menus)	1
Chart (full menus)	2
No active window	3
Info window	4
Worksheet or macro sheet (short menus)	5
Chart (short menus)	6

STEP( )
Single-steps through a macro

STEP starts single-step processing of a macro, displaying a dialog box for each macro instruction, and letting you choose whether to execute the next instruction, halt the macro, or continue normal processing of the instructions. Single-stepping is particularly useful when debugging a macro.

You can also single-step through a macro by pressing the Esc key while it's running.

TERMINATE(*channel#*)
(For IBM Only) Closes a channel to another application

TERMINATE is the opposite of INITIATE, and closes the channel specified by *channel#*. If TERMINATE is not successful, it returns the error message !VALUE!

WAIT(*serialnumber*)
Stops a macro from running

WAIT suspends execution of a macro for the amount of time specified in date/time value *serialnumber*.

Control Functions
ARGUMENT(*nametext,datatype#,reference.*).
Describes arguments to a macro

The ARGUMENT function lets you use named values as arguments in macro functions. These named values will be used wherever the name is referenced in a function macro.

Nametext is the name you want to assign to the argument. It may also be the name of the cells containing the argument, if you're using reference.

Datatype# is a code number specifying the type of entry. (See the INPUT function explanation for *datatype#* values.)

Reference tells *Excel* where you want it to store the value that will be passed to the macro.

BREAK( )
Gets out of a FOR-NEXT or WHILE-NEXT loop

When BREAK is encountered, processing of a FOR-NEXT or WHILE-NEXT loop stops, and macro execution returns to the statement following the NEXT statement at the end of the current loop.

FOR(*counter,start#,end#,increment*)
Starts a FOR-NEXT loop

A loop in a macro allows you to perform some set of actions a finite number of times. A loop means that a set of instructions is repeated, usually with one or more changes to some counter or other variable, until some specified condition occurs.

Looping is a bit like doing situps as part of an exercise program: You repeat the situp exercise each time until you've completed a certain number, and then you can stop and go on to something else.

A FOR statement begins the loop and a NEXT statement marks the end of the loop and the point at which control either returns to the loop if the end-condition hasn't been yet met, or proceeds with statements outside the loop. Loop processing starts at the beginning point and goes to the last statement before the NEXT statement. When the end condition has been met, processing is allowed to get past the NEXT statement.

Arguments that are needed with a FOR-NEXT loop:

Counter is the name of the variable that counts the number of times the loop has been performed; when its value exceeds that of end#, control passes outside of the loop.

219

Start# is optional. It's assumed to be 1 unless otherwise specified. Start# is the value to which counter is set when the loop begins.

End# is the value against which countername is compared after each iteration of the loop. Until the value in countername is greater than end, looping continues.

Increment is the value by which counter is incremented on each pass through the loop.

GOTO(*reference*)
Jumps to another cell

The GOTO function works the same as pressing F5, in that it tells Excel to jump to the upper left cell in reference and continue processing there.

Reference must be a cell or cell range on an open macro sheet, though it doesn't have to be the same macro sheet as the one on which the GOTO statement occurs.

HALT( )
Stops one or more macros from running

HALT stops all macro action. It's particularly useful for stopping processing when an error occurs.

When you use HALT, you should combine it with some function that produces a message, so the user knows why everything has stopped.

NEXT( )
Ends a FOR-NEXT or WHILE-NEXT loop

NEXT is the last statement in a loop. It marks the point at which control either returns to loop processing, or continues on to other instructions, depending on the current state of the counter. (See FOR and WHILE.)

RESTART(*level#*)
Removes return addresses from the stack

When you jump from the middle of one macro to the beginning of another, Excel stores the address of the last instruction in the macro you left as the return address. If you then jump from the second macro to a third, it keeps track of that return address as well. That list of return adresses is known as a *stack*.

When you want to return to the calling macro, *Excel* consults this stack. A level 1 return means control returns to the macro that directly called the macro you're in. If, however, you want to return to some other macro that was in the chain of nested calls, you need to specify a different level.

You may, however, wish to remove some return addresses from that stack. RESTART lets you do that by level number, where level 1 is the most recent call, level 2 is the call or set of calls before that, and so forth. If the *level* argument is omitted, *Excel* removes all return addresses from the stack. Thus, when a RETURN function is encountered, the macro will stop running instead of returning control to the macro that called it.

RESULT(*type#*)
Specifies the data type of a function macro's return value

RESULT is usually used at the beginning of a macro to specify what kind of return value is expected. The kind of return value is specified by a code number:

Type#	Data type
1	Number
2	Text
4	Logical
8	Reference
16	Error
64	Array

Type# can be a sum of the codes, indicating that a combination of types is allowable. For instance, if *type#* = 7 (the default), the return value may be a number, text, or a logical value.

RETURN(*value*)
Returns control to whatever started the macro

RETURN is normally the last instruction in a function or command macro, and tells *Excel* that control is to return to whatever

221

called the macro. This may be the user (using the Macro Run command or a shortcut key), a formula, or another macro.

Use of the *value* argument depends on whether the macro is a command macro or a function macro. In a command macro run by the user, don't specify *value*. In a function macro, value specifies the return value associated with this macro.

WHILE(*testvalue*)
Starts a WHILE-NEXT loop

WHILE begins a loop of instructions that ends with a NEXT statement. WHILE continues to loop until *testvalue* is FALSE, unlike a FOR-NEXT loop, where the exit from the loop is determined by a counter.

If *testvalue* is FALSE the first time, execution skips to the matching NEXT instruction and proceeds with the instruction after it.

Value-Returning Functions

ABSREF(*referencetext,reference*)
Returns the absolute reference of a cell

ABSREF lets you determine the reference of one cell by describing its position relative to another cell. *Referencetext* must be in R1C1-style, a relative reference, and in text form: "R[− 2]C[− 2]". If *reference* is a cell range, *referencetext* is assumed to be relative to the upper left corner of *reference*.

Examples

ABSREF("R[− 2]C[− 2]",D5) = B3
ABSREF("R[− 1]C[− 1]",D10:E150 = C9

ACTIVE.CELL( )
Returns the reference of the active cell

ACTIVE.CELL returns the reference of the active cell as an external reference. ACTIVE.CELL is particularly useful when you're working with linked worksheets and need to communicate the value or position of the active cell to an external file.

Normally the value returned by ACTIVE.CELL will be the value contained in the active cell, since that's how it's usually translated. If you want the reference instead, use REFTEXT to convert the active cell reference to text, which can then be stored or manipulated.

CALLER( )
Returns the reference of the cell that started the function macro

Unlike RETURN, CALLER returns the reference of the cell that contained the function that called the currently running macro. If the function was part of an array formula, CALLER returns the range reference. If the currently running macro is a command macro started by the user, CALLER returns the error message #REF!.

DEREF(*reference*)
Returns the value of a cell in a reference

In most cases, a reference to a cell returns the value of that cell. If, however, you have used a function such as SET.NAME, references are not always converted to values.

In those cases, the DEREF function returns a value. If *reference* is the reference of a single cell, DEREF returns the value of that cell. If the reference is a range of cells, DEREF returns the array of values in those cells.

DOCUMENTS( )
Returns the names of open documents

DOCUMENT returns the names of all open files in alphabetical order as an aray of text values. It's frequently used with INDEX to select individual file names for other uses.

FILES(*directoryname*)
Returns the names of files in a specific directory

FILES gives you a horizontal text array of the filenames in the directory you specify. You can use the wildcard characters * and ? in the FILES argument. Up to 256 filenames can be returned. If *directoryname* is not specified, it's assumed to be *.*.

223

GET.BAR( )
Returns the number of the active menu bar

Built-in menu bar numbers are:

Number	Built-in Menu Bar
1	Worksheet and macro menu, full menus
2	Chart menu, full menus
3	Nil menu (menu displayed when no documents are open)
4	Info window menu
5	Worksheet and macro menu, short menus
6	Chart menu, short menus

GET.CELL(*infocode,reference*)
Returns information about a cell

GET.CELL tells you about the location, contents, or formatting of the upper left cell in *reference*. If *reference* is omitted, it's assumed to be the current selection.

The argument *infocode* specifies what kind of information you want:

Infocode	Result
1	Reference of upper left cell in area specified, as text
2	Row number of the top cell in reference
3	Column number of the leftmost cell in reference
4	The same as TYPE(reference)
5	Contents of reference
6	The formula in reference, as text
7	Format of cell, as text
8	Cell's alignment:
	1 = General
	2 = Left
	3 = Center
	4 = Right
	5 = Fill

Infocode	Result
9	If cell has left border, returns TRUE; otherwise FALSE
10	If cell has right border, returns TRUE; otherwise FALSE
11	If cell has top border, returns TRUE; otherwise FALSE
12	If cell has bottom border, returns TRUE; otherwise FALSE
13	If cell is shaded, returns TRUE; otherwise FALSE
14	If cell is locked, returns TRUE; otherwise FALSE
15	If cell is hidden, returns TRUE; otherwise FALSE
16	Column width of the cell, measured in characters of Font 1
17	Row height of cell, in points
18	Name of font, as text
19	Size of font, in points
20	If cell is bold, returns TRUE; otherwise FALSE
21	If cell is italic, returns TRUE; otherwise FALSE
22	If cell is underlined, returns TRUE; otherwise FALSE
23	If cell is overstruck, returns TRUE; otherwise FALSE

GET.CHART.ITEM(*xyindex, pointindex, code*)

Returns the location of a chart element in a chart window

This function returns the vertical or horizontal position of a point on a chart element. The argument *xyindex* is a code number: 1 for horizontal coordinate of the position, or 2 for the vertical coordinate.

Pointindex specifies the point on the chart object, as shown below. If the selected object is a point, *pointindex* must be 1. If *pointindex* is omitted, it is assumed to be 1.

The value given for *code* is in text form, and is the same as shown under SELECT, discussed earlier.

If the selected object is any line other than a data line, these values are used for *pointindex*:

Pointindex	Chart Object Position
1	Lower left
2	Upper right

If the selected object is a rectangle or an area in an area chart, these values are used for *pointindex*:

225

Pointindex	Chart Object Position
1	Upper left
2	Upper middle
3	Upper right
4	Right middle
5	Lower right
6	Lower middle
7	Lower left
8	Lower middle

If the selected object is an arrow, these values are used for *pointindex:*

Pointindex	Chart Object Position
1	Base
2	Head

If the selected object is a pie slice, these values are used for *pointindex:*

Pointindex	Chart Object Position
1	Outermost counterclockwise point
2	Outer center point
3	Outermost clockwise point
4	Midpoint of the most clockwise radius
5	Center point
6	Midpoint of the most counterclockwise radius

GET.DEF(*definition, document*)
Returns a name matching a definition

Returns the text version of the name that matches whatever is in *definition*, which may be a part of *document*. *Definition* may be a reference, but if so, must be in R1C1 style.

GET.DOCUMENT(*infotype, nametext*)
Returns information about a document

GET.DOCUMENT(*infotype,nametext*)

Returns information about a document

Depending on the code you specify in *infotype*,
GET.DOCUMENT returns information about the document you
identify in *nametext*. If *nametext* is omitted, it is assumed to be the
active document.

Infotype	Result
1	Name of the document as text; does not include drive, directory, or window number.
2	Path name of directory containing *nametext*. If *nametext* has not yet been saved, returns the error message #N/A!.
3	Returns:
	1 If the document is a worksheet.
	2 If the document is a chart.
	3 If the document is a macro sheet.
	4 If the active window is the Info window.
4	TRUE if changes have been made to the document since it was last saved; FALSE if no changes have been made.
5	TRUE if access is read-only; FALSE otherwise.
6	TRUE if file is protected; FALSE otherwise.
7	TRUE of contents are protected; FALSE otherwise.
8	TRUE if document windows are protected; FALSE otherwise.

The four *infotypes* shown below apply only to charts:

Infotype	Result
9	Code number indicating type of chart:
	1 Area
	2 Bar
	3 Column
	4 Line
	5 Pie
	6 Scatter
10	Code number (same as above) indicating type of overlay chart. If there is no overlay chart, returns #N/A!.

Infotype	Result
11	Number of series in main chart.
12	Number of series in overlay chart.

The remaining *infotype* values apply only to worksheets and macro sheets:

Infotype	Result
9	Row number of first row used. If document is empty, returns 0.
10	Row number of last row used. If document is empty, returns 0.
11	Column number of first column used. If document is empty, returns 0.
12	Column number of last column used. If document is empty, returns 0.
13	Number of windows.
14	Code number indicating calculation mode:
	1 Automatic
	2 Automatic except tables
	3 Manual
15	TRUE if iteration is enabled; otherwise FALSE.
16	Maximum number of iterations.
17	Maximum change between iterations.
18	TRUE if updating remote reference is enabled; FALSE otherwise.
19	TRUE if set to Precision as Displayed; FALSE otherwise.
20	TRUE is document is using 1904 date system; FALSE otherwise.
21	Four-item horizontal text array of the names of the four fonts.
22	Four-item horizontal number array of the sizes of the four fonts.

GET.FORMULA(*reference*)

Returns the contents of a cell

GET.FORMULA returns the contents of *reference* as it would appear in the formula bar. The contents are returned as text. If the formula contains references, they are returned in R1C1-style.

GET.NAME(*nametext*)

Returns the definition of a name

GET.NAME returns a name's definition as it would appear in the Refers to text box Formula Define Name command. *Nametext* can be a name on a macro sheet, or an external reference to a name defined on a document.

If the definition of *nametext* contains references, they're returned in R1C1-style.

GET.NOTE(*cellreference, start, count*)

Returns characters from a note

GET.NOTE returns count number of characters from the cell identified by *cellreference,* beginning at the character numbered *start.* If *start* is omitted, it is assumed to be 1. If *count* is omitted, it is assumed to be the length of the note attached to *cellreference.*

GET.WINDOW(*infotype, nametext*)

Returns information about a window

Depending on the code you specify in *infotype,* GET.WINDOW returns information about the window you identify in *nametext.* If *nametext* is omitted, it's assumed to be the active window.

Use *infotype* to specify what kind of information you want. *Infotypes* 1 through 7 apply to all windows, and 8 through 17 apply to worksheets and macro sheets. *Infotypes* 13 through 17 return numeric arrays that specify what rows or columns are at the edges of the panes in the specified window.

Infotype	Results
1	Name of document in the window specified in nametext, as text.
2	Number of window specified
3	Number of points from the left edge of your screen to the left edge of the window (*x* position)
4	Number of points from the top edge of your screen to the top edge of the window (*y* position)
5	Width, measured in points
6	Height, measured in points
7	TRUE if window is hidden; otherwise FALSE
8	TRUE if formulas are displayed; otherwise FALSE
9	TRUE if gridlines are displayed; otherwise FALSE
10	TRUE if row and column headings are displayed; otherwise FALSE

Infotype	Results
11	TRUE if 0s are displayed; otherwise FALSE
12	Code number 0–8 giving the color of gridlines and headlines, corresponding to colors shown in the Options Display dialog box. (0 is equivalent to the Automatic Display option.)
13	The leftmost column of each pane, as an array
14	The top row of each pane, as an array
15	The rightmost column of each pane, as an array
16	The bottom row of each pane, as an array
17	Returns the active pane number

GET.WORKSPACE(*infotype*)

Returns information about the workspace

Depending on the code you specify in *infotype,* GET.WORKSPACE returns information about your workspace. Use *infotype* to specify what kind of information you want.

Infotype	Result
1	Name and version number of the environment in which *Excel* is running, as text
2	Version number of *Excel,* as text
3	If auto-decimal is set, returns the number of decimals; otherwise 0
4	TRUE if in R1C1 mode; FALSE if in A1 mode
5	TRUE if scroll bars are displayed; otherwise FALSE
6	TRUE if status bar is displayed; otherwise FALSE
7	TRUE if formula bar is displayed; otherwise FALSE
8	TRUE if remote requests are enabled; otherwise FALSE
9	Returns alternate menu key as text; returns #N/A! if no alternate menu key is set
10	Special mode code number: 1 Data Find 2 Copy 3 Cut 0 No special mode
11	Number of points from the left edge of your screen to the left edge of the *Excel* window (*x* position)

Infotype	Result
12	Number of points from the top edge of your screen to the top edge of the *Excel* window (*y* position)
13	Usable workspace width, in points
14	Usable workspace height, in points
15	Maximize/minimize code number:
	1 *Excel* is neither maximized nor minimized
	2 Minimized
	3 Maximized
16	Number of K of memory free
17	Total number of K of memory available to *Excel*
18	TRUE if math coprocessor is present; otherwise FALSE
19	TRUE if mouse is present; otherwise FALSE

LINKS(*docname*)

Returns the names of all linked documents

LINKS returns a horizontal array of the names of all documents referred to by external references in the document specified by *docname*. If *docname* is omitted, it is assumed to be the active document. If the document identified by *docname* contains no external references, LINKS returns the error message #N/A!.

NAMES(*docname*)

Returns an array of defined names on a document

NAMES returns a horizontal text array of all names that are defined on *docname*. If *docname* is omitted, it is assumed to be the active document.

OFFSET(*reference, rows, columns, height, width*)

Returns a reference offset from a given reference

OFFSET returns the reference *height* rows high and *width* columns wide that is *rows* rows and *columns* columns offset from *reference*. If *height* or *width* are omitted, they're assumed to have the same dimensions as *reference*.

If the offset parameters go over the edge of the worksheet, OFFSET returns the #REF! error message. If *reference* is a multiple value, the function returns the error message #VALUE!.

REFTEXT(*reference,a1*)

Converts a reference into text

Converts *reference* to an absolute reference, as text. If *a1* is TRUE, REFTEXT returns it in A1-style; if FALSE or omitted, REFTEXT returns it in R1C1-style.

RELREF(*reference,comparison*)

Returns a relative reference

RELREF compares *comparison* to *reference* and returns a relative reference, in R1C1-style, as text.

Example

RELREF(B3,C4) = "R[− 1]C[− 1]"

SELECTION( )

Returns the reference of a selection

SELECTION returns the reference of a selection as an external reference.

Normally the value returned by SELECTION is converted to a value rather than stored as a reference. If you want the reference rather than the value, use REFTEXT to convert the reference to text, which can then be further manipulated.

TEXTREF(*text,a1*)

Converts text to a reference

Converts the *text* specified to a cell reference. If *a1* is TRUE, *text* is assumed to be in A1-style; if *a1* is FALSE or omitted, *text* is assumed to be in R1C1-style.

WINDOWS( )

Returns the names of open windows

WINDOWS returns a horizontal text array of all windows on your screen, in order by level. The active window is the first named; the window directly under that is the second, and so forth.

Index